THE ART OF THINKING

THE ART OF THINKING

How the Great Philosophers Can Stimulate Our Ability to Think Critically

By José Carlos Ruiz

Translated from Spanish by **Ezra E. Fitz**

DIVERSION
BOOKS

Diversion Books
A division of Diversion Publishing Corp.
www.diversionbooks.com

For more information, email info@diversionbooks.com

Originally published in Spanish as *El arte de pensar* by Editorial Almuzara, November 2018
First Diversion Books Edition: May 2026
Trade Paperback ISBN: 979-8-89515-098-6
e-ISBN: 979-8-89515-099-3

Design by Westchester Publishing Services
Cover design by Jen Huppert

Printed in the United States of America
1 3 5 7 9 10 8 6 4 2

To my children, Pedro and Elena:
Celebration and Refuge

Contents

	Introduction	1
CHAPTER 1	Preventive Mental Hygiene	7
CHAPTER 2	Critical Thinking: The Hidden Beauty of Happiness	12
CHAPTER 3	Curiosity	17
CHAPTER 4	The Grass and the Tree	24
CHAPTER 5	Pascal and Spinoza: The Joy of Improving	28
CHAPTER 6	Kant: Fools and Cowards	36
CHAPTER 7	Socrates: Good People	52
CHAPTER 8	Daniel Bernoulli: How to Make Good Decisions	57
CHAPTER 9	Barry Schwartz: The Burden of Having to Choose	63
CHAPTER 10	Lipovetsky: The Value of Contradiction	74
CHAPTER 11	Victoria Camps: Post-Truth and In Praise of Doubt	81

CHAPTER 12 Pyrrho of Elis: Pragmatic Skepticism 87
CHAPTER 13 Montaigne: Self-Esteem, or Thinking Highly of Oneself 93
CHAPTER 14 Solid Thinking: The Importance of Context 100
CHAPTER 15 Ortega y Gasset: Circumstance for the Twenty-First Century 104
CHAPTER 16 Aristotle: How to Control Anxiety 115
CHAPTER 17 Living for Success 122
CHAPTER 18 Diogenes of Sinope: Thinking and Living in Coherence 127
CHAPTER 19 The Kingdom of Manichaeanism 139
CHAPTER 20 Alain de Botton: Snobbery and the Obsession with Labeling 151
CHAPTER 21 Martin Luther and the American Dream: Work as a Swindle 155
CHAPTER 22 Hephaestus and Aphrodite: Thinking about Merit, or the Merits of Thinking 163
CHAPTER 23 Amancio Ortega: The Virus of False Hope 171
CHAPTER 24 Bertrand Russell: Thinking about Envy and Misfortune 176
CHAPTER 25 Against Emotional Fragility 192
CHAPTER 26 Hobbes: Critical Thinking against Fear 197
CHAPTER 27 Hellenistic Schools: Instructions for Times of Crisis 201
CHAPTER 28 Seneca: How to Think about Anger 218
Conclusion 225
Bibliography 227

Although culture in general is no guarantee for living better or having more reasonable life plans, to underestimate it is to lack the weapons with which to confront the brutality we all carry within ourselves.

—Victoria Camps

Introduction

Who could have thought that, in the twenty-first century, happiness would become an instrument of torture? We are now burdened by a curse that goes unnoticed by most people: the curse of happiness. We've been condemned to be happy not only as an obligation but also—and more concerning—through intimidation. And it has happened in such a subtle and sophisticated way that we've come to believe it's our idea. It has been suggested to us that we should feel happy, but notice the difference between feeling happy and being happy. This tyranny is based on a self-serving concept of sentimental, emotional, and lighthearted happiness: something instantaneous and easy to acquire. We've been turned into emotional drug addicts. And our punishment is clear: Sentenced to a life of injecting ourselves with this false sense of happiness, we fall into a constant search for hits in any form, all of which fall under the buzzword of the day—*trends*. These trends are linked to experiential consumption, because what sells these days are experiences, feelings that disturb us, unsettle us, excite us, sensations capable of altering our mood and which, mind you, are always associated with positive emotions. New doses are designed daily, each more appealing than the last, and the offerings are so substantial and stimulating that it's impossible to try them all.

The curse consists in wanting to savor each and every one of these doses, which is precisely why we've fallen into this perverse trap: hyperaction, hyperactivity. To avoid developing hypermodern withdrawal symptoms, we try to consume as many portions as possible. Knowing this, the System itself encourages us to follow a checklist-like policy. It spurs us on, driving us to maintain our lists so we can check off each and every dose we consume: trendy restaurants, can't-miss trips, the latest gadget to hit the market, those awesome Zumba/yoga/boxing classes, mindfulness sessions, enjoying a Friday brunch, getting a tattoo, being a hipster, a marathoner, a vegan. All we have to do is cross off each dose from the list we consume, but not before posting it on Facebook or Instagram.

Since the range of doses offered is so vast, the System can keep us busy, hooked, and subjected to incessant activity, to hyperactivity. To make matters worse, we know that many of these doses come with an expiration date, so anxiety sets in as time runs out. Condemned to never stop, to never even slow down. Obsessed with individually wrapped packets of happiness. The System has managed to create a popular, ready-made notion of instant, highly soluble happiness linked to hyper-consumption, both in emotional and material terms. To stop, to pause, to reflect is to agonize. As Hamlet, prince of Denmark, famously said, "To die, to sleep."

Reflection has been taken over by the dictatorship of action, and it is now more urgent than ever to revive critical thinking before it takes its last breath. Because, in this turbo-temporal society, in this cult of instantaneousness, of prioritizing immediacy, critical thinking will always—eventually—come into play.

Sooner or later, analysis, study, and reflection will appear in our lives, and in many cases, they will be accompanied by suffering due to our failure (or unwillingness) to think critically. For this, there is no consolation. No matter how we live our lives under this paradigm of hyperactivity, reflection will always show up, knocking at our door, disturbing us like an inconvenient guest who shows up in the middle of a peaceful night, catching us disoriented, off guard, and with nothing in the fridge to offer.

The ability to think well, like any other valuable skill, is an art, and it requires many hours of work and effort to polish and refine it before it can be showcased in all its splendor. It's also worth noting that it is currently in danger of extinction, gradually fading away with few seeming to notice.

In a subtle and, if I might say, almost elegant way, the System—free market capitalism—has committed the perfect crime. What's remarkable about this crime is that it won't make the headlines, nor will there be a funeral for the victim, in part because no one will suspect that the victim has died. This lack of suspicion is understandable, because the System has managed to quash its own worst enemy: critical thinking. To do so, it has thrown up smoke screens, diverting attention to other adversaries and problems (antiestablishmentism, posthumanism, fundamentalism, terrorism, climate change, the economic crisis, the robotization of daily life, etc.), while quietly leaving critical thinking moribund and replacing it with a facsimile the System manipulates at will.

In much the same way that it has remotely directed society's attention toward these adversaries and problems, the System has also developed a series of alliances to serve its purpose: Alliances that have created the perfect conditions so that nobody misses the Legitimate. We don't miss it because the System itself has built a virtual replica and presented it as real, a puppet whose strings are always being pulled in the same direction by the same hands. And, of course, the artifice of this virtual Critical Thinking is presented so realistically that we fail to notice the authentic one is lying in a state near death. This pretender has usurped the throne of the Genuine and now commands the direction in which society must move. It focuses attention on the human being's emotional axis in order to build a collective that is intellectually anesthetized, yet self-absorbed in a distorted notion of happiness.

As this is happening, society submits in sibylline fashion to the rule of emotions and hyperactivity, driven by an army of allies including acceleration, drive, passion, vocation, enthusiasm, mindfulness, coaching, meditation, yoga—many of which are activities to be performed within a specific period, thus negating the possibility they will become habits—while indirectly weakening critical thinking and creating the necessary circumstance for preventing its development. The consequence of this crime is one we are suffering firsthand: imbalance.

Balance is the primary mechanism underpinning an individual's development, and the only way to maintain it is through critical thinking. Knowing this, economic liberalism has launched a strategy of harassment and dismantling aimed at weakening it as much as possible. The implication is obvious: we live in an unbalanced society. The scales between reason and emotion have definitely tipped in favor of the latter. Through this strategy, the System has achieved two things. The first is that we no longer realize that we are unbalanced, while the second (which is a consequence of the first) is the ostracism and oblivion to which we have relegated critical thinking.

Since antiquity, the goal has been to educate balanced individuals who are capable of understanding and controlling their emotions while simultaneously having the ability to do the same with their peers. Even Plato, in his myth of the charioteer, illustrated the need for the driver, representing the human being's rationality, to be able to guide his chariot toward the World of Ideas. To do this, he must be able to control both the human being's ignoble passions (the black horse) and its noble ones (the white horse). Not surprisingly, his most esteemed disciple, Aristotle, defined virtuous behavior (the act of achieving virtue) as that which is attained by following, as a point of reference, the golden mean. The attainment of balance. These two thinkers, despite their diverging philosophies, agreed that the only way to achieve critical thinking was through its proper use.

Along with this worship of the proper use of thought, both engaged in a fierce struggle against the world of opinion and belief, though each with its own methodology. Plato was an enemy of projected images—in his case, those found on the walls deep inside a cave—and established Episteme, Knowledge, as the level of understanding to which we must aspire. Aristotle went so far as to claim that what distinguishes us from other living beings is the use of speech. In his attempt to define the human being's idiosyncrasy, Plato's disciple developed a theory of happiness based on the proper use of reason:

> "That man is much more a political animal than any kind of bee or any herd animal is clear. For, as we assert, nature does nothing in vain; and man alone among the animals has speech."
>
> —*Politics*, Book I

And yet here we are, living in a world where the image has triumphed over the word, where the ever-present screen has invaded each and every corner of our daily lives, charting the course of future reason and replacing the word as the fount of analysis. Therefore, it is essential that we immediately get to work if we want to revive what once best defined us as a species: Critical Thinking.

ONE

Preventive Mental Hygiene

There are plenty of self-help books on the market, many of which not only tell us we can achieve any goal we set for ourselves—happiness included—but also show us how to do it. Others address the suffering that overwhelms us when we don't succeed. It's a self-sustaining business. We write a bunch of motivational books in which we tell people it's all just a matter of effort, perseverance, emotion, passion . . . and then, when they do what those books prescribe and fail to achieve their goals, they buy a new set of books on personal growth that explain how to deal with the sadness and discouragement they feel when they fail. Why does this happen? Most of the time, it's because they're telling us how to act without taking us into account. Other times, we are the ones who fail due to a lack of willpower, to an inability to put the advice they offer us into practice.

True help doesn't lie in doing what others tell us to do, but rather in learning to develop critical thinking for ourselves, based on our own circumstance, from our own perspectives, and while making the most appropriate decisions while always taking context into account.

As we will try to clarify, critical thinking is based on two key elements that we must master if we want to utilize it properly: circumstance and context. Because the art of knowing how to think critically comes down to understanding the circumstances that surround both ourselves and others and knowing how to interpret that context correctly. Once we understand and master these two tools, decisions regarding the projection of our life that we wish to pursue will have a greater chance of success.

Throughout this book, we will demonstrate how what's commonly referred to as critical thinking can be used to achieve a grounded, balanced, and happy presence. The difference is a crucial one. Thinking critically—that is, possessing strong analytical skills—is an essential tool for forging one's own true, authentic identity. It doesn't have to do with laying out what needs to be done; rather, it's about reflecting on our philosophy of life, on our way of thinking about the life we're leading. It's about doing this internally while also remembering that we must apply this reflection onto others.

More than a few Spanish speakers around the globe have embraced the famous saying "*más feliz que una perdiz*" (which means something along the lines of "happy as a lark"), but if we dig deeper into the meaning of this expression, we'll see soon enough that it doesn't have any particular significance, that it doesn't carry any underlying wisdom. One might assume that the *perdiz*, or partridge, is happier compared to other birds, but unfortunately, that's not the case. The *perdiz* was chosen simply because it rhymed: *feliz / perdiz*. Some were adventurous enough to rhyme *feliz* with *lombris* (a worm), yet when a foreigner tries to find a translation for this expression and investigate its origin, they're in for a big letdown, because there's no interesting backstory from which to glean anything. It's all so simple, so obvious, as inconsistent as it is empty. There was a need for a word in Spanish that rhymed with "happy," and the partridge fit the bill.

In some theories about the expression, it dates back to another common phrase from the fairy tales of yore which, in Spanish, ended with "*fueron felices y comieron perdices*" (which is akin to "they lived happily ever after, eating partridges"), because the bird was considered a delicacy by the wealthy and therefore a symbol of material prosperity. In fact, in countries like France, there are partridge hatcheries for those with sufficient purchasing power. If we follow the logical progression of this matter, it is indeed possible that the expression stems from this.

For all this time, we've been led to understand that living happily ever after and feasting on partridges is a précis for what it means to live a good life—a life of luxury—in which happiness is associated with economic prosperity—a life of nobility—and we end up reducing our wellness to a monetary figure that's as stark as it is concise. But since happiness tied to material consumption will always raise moral suspicions, the System, thanks to a little sleight of hand, has shifted the focus onto another standard of joy that's less susceptible to immorality: that of emotional consumption.

When we talk about happiness, we're using the word in a simplistic way, in an overly cheerful manner, without fully understanding what all it entails. We associate happiness with emotions and feelings, and in doing so we make the mistake of not associating it with reason. This is a common error, one that results from not stopping to think, from not flipping the critical thinking switch that comes with the standard package of our make and model as human beings. To understand what happiness is, we need to think analytically about patterns in our lives, and it must be done from the perspective of our circumstance, from our reality.

We can argue that happiness is a way of being, a way of thinking and feeling about life, one that can be learned. To that point, the conclusions of a longitudinal experiment—that is, one conducted over time while using the same group of individuals—assessing their level of happiness throughout their lives was published. Produced by the Harvard Study of Adult Development, this research project began in 1938 and examined the lives of seven hundred men in an attempt to analyze the factors that resulted in some people aging happily and healthily while others ended up unhappy and suffering from cognitive decline. Two completely different groups of twenty-year-olds were chosen: on one side, nearly three hundred Harvard students, and on the other, some four hundred young men from a poor neighborhood in Boston. It's a detailed study that is still ongoing and has expanded to include their families, wives, children, and even grandchildren. Can one imagine what would happen if they could isolate the traits that provide us with a happy and healthy life? Well, among the data they collected about personal wellness and personal health, they concluded that relationships with friends and partners were crucial. According to this study, the key lies in having good social relationships. Thus, when people retire and replace the sociability of work with that of other friends, their levels of health and happiness remain intact. As the current director of the study, Dr. Robert Waldinger, said:

> "Over and over, over these seventy-five years, our study has shown that the people who fared the best were the people who leaned in to relationships, with family, with friends, with community."

An important part of happiness lies not only in relationships with others (as opposed to isolation) but in intelligent relationships, the kind that take into consideration the way people should be treated, that involve true affection, which itself stems from the proper use of intelligence. This means learning to observe others as well as ourselves, analyzing the context and circumstances that surround us, while also taking into account and understanding the circumstances surrounding others.

Knowing what others need to be happy—to feel good, to feel secure—and providing that for them is a sign of supreme intelligence. It demonstrates that we're able to use critical thinking effectively, because happiness is a way of being in life that involves knowing how to think properly in order to distinguish between the things that benefit us and those that cause us harm.

TWO

Critical Thinking: The Hidden Beauty of Happiness

Learning to think seems easy enough because we all do it. The question, then, is do we do it well? When we talk about raising a child, we worry a lot about things that seem essential to their development: whether they play sports, eat healthy food, fulfill their obligations at school. . . . We sign them up for extracurricular activities to teach or reinforce things we consider extremely important, but it never occurs to us that we could be enrolling them in reasoning classes or other exercises to boost their critical thinking skills and enhance their ability to think positively. It never ceases to amaze how much we obsess over whether our children are staying in shape, taking care to avoid illness, or their learning development. We have regular medical checkups to ensure that everything is progressing and developing as they should. But at no point do we ever reflect on patterns of thought or philosophies of life. We hardly ever stop to think about whether we have a sensible life plan in place or if we're projecting an appropriate set of ideals onto our children in order to develop a balanced personality.

We've managed to assimilate the concept of "preventive medicine," in which we understand the importance of healthy lifestyle habits in order to age well and prevent and/or detect diseases as early as possible. We diet and exercise because we want to look good and shed those few extra pounds, but when it comes to our ideas, desires, and concerns, we don't think there's anything to get rid of, and we don't do what Robert Zimmer calls "mental gymnastics." Starting at a young age, we do a lot of physical exercise to develop proper psychomotor skills and grow healthily, but when it comes to mental exercise, we presume, almost innately, that it simply comes as part of the package. And, of course, what we have happening are sculpted bodies, forty-somethings with barely any body fat showing off their abs, yet loaded up on antianxiety pills and antidepressants to cope with the lifestyles they've built based on a foundational way of thinking that is neither critical nor autonomous, and which—most of the time—they have no control over.

We undertake Herculean feats of willpower to avoid eating, drinking, or consuming things that we crave, because we know they're harmful to our bodies. We use that willpower to exercise when what we'd rather do after we get home is sit back in our recliners and turn on an episode of our favorite TV show. But when it comes to learning how to think, to analyzing the preconceived ideas we've assimilated, to understanding other people's points of view, that same willpower vanishes because "stopping to think" feels tiresome or annoying to us.

We need to learn to think critically at a young age so as to analyze not just our ideas but even more so our beliefs, our desires, our dreams. . . . We must teach our children as well as ourselves to ask the right questions and to know when they/we need to flip the critical thinking switch.

Philosophy can be a great asset in this task. It's a mental activity that can be practiced at any age and honed as one learns to shed the prejudices and bad habits accumulated throughout life. Habits that, ultimately, are nothing more than those few extra pounds that keep us from moving freely, from navigating life with greater ease, and from facing day-to-day challenges. If we do this well, then both our children/students and ourselves will enjoy the most important element for living a happy life: mental hygiene.

The twenty-first-century question we must be asking ourselves is this: Why don't we take care of our critical thinking the same way we take care of our bodies? We've managed to introduce the concept of "Preventive Medicine," which saves us a lot of suffering and discomfort and wards off premature deaths, but we haven't gone beyond that. Now, the great unmet obligation is to do the same with mental hygiene, to have preventive mental hygiene, to create healthy mental habits that will serve us in avoiding a miserable life.

A bad mental habit, like a false sense of success or harmful notion of happiness, can cause greater suffering than physical, biological ailments. Yet despite knowing this, we do nothing to prevent it from happening to us or to our loved ones. When I use the word "miserable," I'm not referring to financial misery but rather to feelings of misfortune, to feeling like an unfortunate person. As with any worthwhile hygienic cleansing, mental hygiene will help us eliminate the viral ideas that have infected us, spread through us, and caused—in the most extreme cases—immense pain to the point that our very will to live is curtailed. Without good mental hygiene, we can succumb to very unhealthy thinking habits that may seem harmless and innocuous at first, but which always end up exacting a long-term toll and diminishing the quality of our lives.

Critical thinking can be learned at a young age. It's akin to the smoker who decides to quit at forty-five after having smoked since the person was twenty. Ideally, the person would never have started smoking in the first place, but the good thing about critical thinking is that it can be put into practice at any stage of life. What's obvious, of course, is that it will be harder at this age because the person will have to shake off bad mental habits acquired over the years. But the good thing about people who decide to quit smoking is that, in time, the body's regenerative powers are unmatched. In this book, we will attempt to show that mental hygiene can be achieved, and that it is possible to both explain it and learn it through the particulars of everyday life.

There are no shortcuts along the path to learning how to think, just as there are no shortcuts to the goal of being happy. There aren't any because one cannot be happy without being able to think properly. Happiness is a way of being. It is cultivated row by row, it must be tended to daily, and then, inevitably, it will bear fruit. Learning to think well is the same. It must be done slowly and gradually until, in time, it becomes a habit that will help us to achieve a balanced life and develop a strong personality.

Happiness isn't just an emotion. It's not something instantaneous that brings a smile to our faces at a random moment. Happiness is something greater than a feeling; it's deeper, more rooted, more established. It's a way of being into which we wake up each and every morning, which is precisely why it must be nurtured at every step along the way so that the seed we sow can take root, anchoring itself within us until it blossoms, transforming us into people who are and feel truly happy.

It is possible to be happy, but like many truly important things in life, it takes a great deal of time and energy to achieve.

But the possibility of finding happiness does exist as long as one is willing to learn how to do so, and for that to happen, we must develop critical thinking skills as quickly as possible, from the most frivolous and perhaps even superficial matters to the issues that distress us the most. Like anything else, it's simply a matter of getting down to work.

One cannot be happy without the ability to think properly. Many people feign happiness: smiling, looking perfectly photogenic in their selfies, blithely projecting a virtual image of bliss, and constantly keeping themselves occupied with exciting activities while simultaneously taking medications to combat the feelings of emptiness that plague them. Every once in a while, they might catch a fleeting moment of joy on a trip abroad, while dining at a chic restaurant, or catching a show on Broadway or the Gran Vía, which they might—without even realizing it—mistake for true happiness.

It's not about learning to be optimistic just for the sake of it. That's not what we're talking about here. It's about learning to construct a lifestyle whose foundation is rooted in happiness and which is understood as a way of being.

THREE

Curiosity

Professor and philosophical practitioner Lou Marinoff states that, when talking with a patient who is suffering from some malady and is seeking a philosophical therapy that might be helpful, the first step is to try to understand the person's personality type, and based on that, explore the philosophical modes in which the person should feel most comfortable. It's not about imposing but rather investigating and aligning various philosophical viewpoints with those of the patient and analyzing his or her own philosophy of life. We all construct such a philosophy for ourselves, and most of the time we do so without even realizing it. Very few of us reflect upon it. To use the French philosopher Michel Onfray's phrase, "We are all born philosophers, yet only a few are lucky enough to remain so." This quote, to me, always seemed quite fitting when it comes to understanding the world in which we live and the sort of people we are becoming.

One of the benefits of learning to think well—of knowing how to utilize critical thinking—is that it becomes a weapon we can tailor to our needs, a weapon we can carry with us throughout our lives. It's not a matter of simply following advice on what we need to do; rather, it's about building our philosophy of life with the best tool: The weapon we wield to protect ourselves against unhappiness, anxiety, depression, frustration, suffering, or fear—critical thinking.

A weapon can serve multiple functions. First, it can be an instrument of defense against the negative forces manifesting themselves through mass media, through the harassment we're subjected to thanks to the screens we're surrounded by, through harmful thoughts, and through insubstantial ideas. It can serve as a powerful shield against these attacks, especially when it comes to defending ourselves from toxic, manipulative people, including that particular type of individual Jean-Charles Bouchoux so aptly defined as "the narcissistic pervert." So, when this society tries to attack us with countless strategies and with its entire arsenal at its disposal, we can always take refuge in our bunker of critical thinking.

But a weapon also serves as a deterrent against that which might disrupt our sense of peace. When we brandish our own arsenal of ideas, reflections, our philosophy of life grounded in critical thinking, we fend off all those harmful people and ideas that, upon seeing the potential we possess, will immediately retreat, fully cognizant of the futility of their endeavors.

To wield this weapon, we need to know what elements it's made of. We are, of course, born philosophers in the sense that we enter this world filled with wonder, especially during the early stages of life, where everything provokes admiration and intrigue, where we ask ourselves about what surrounds us, about those who surround us.

We inherently carry with us a set of attitudes that are quintessentially associated with philosophy: perplexity and wonder on the one hand, while on the other sits the need to know, the ability to question and challenge—in a word, curiosity. And yet, as the years go by, we enter the realm of the predictable, of the ready-made, TV-dinner version of life, of the tyranny of the immediate, of a turbocharged temporality that makes it increasingly difficult to be surprised by anything at all.

It's important to develop and maintain a sense of curiosity that's as aware and healthy as possible if one is to avoid opening Pandora's box. If we don't protect curiosity under the aegis of critical thinking, we may end up falling into a constant state of anxiety from trying to respond to all the overwhelming stimuli invading us on a daily basis.

The curiosity of children, of infants, is neutral because they have yet to develop the processes of responsibility associated with the consequences of their interest. But things are different when it comes to adults. A child's curiosity is driven by wonder, but with adults it often becomes the driving force behind the pursuit of knowledge. We want to know how something works, how to fix it, how to improve it, how to modify it, and within this thought lies, ultimately, the idea of power. Science draws directly from this adult sense of curiosity. To offer one example, J. Robert Oppenheimer, one of the fathers of the atomic bomb and director of the infamous Manhattan Project, once wrote in his notebook:

> "When you see something that is technically sweet, you go ahead and do it and you argue about what to do about it only after you have had your technical success. That is the way it was with the atomic bomb."

This makes it abundantly clear that an adult's curiosity cannot remain neutral but is, instead, reflective, and it's worth asking whether the fact that something can be done implies that it should be done.

Not long ago, I happened to be at the recording of one of the longest-running shows on Spanish television, *Adventures with Knowledge*, along with Professor Martínez Mojica, an international pioneer in CRISPR-Cas9, the genetic cut-and-paste tool. I asked him about what role ethical responsibility played in his research. He told me that the university had a bioethics committee and explained that, in his role as a researcher, he was developing the technical aspects in collaboration with other international experts. I remember telling him how surprised I was to discover that the current National Bioethics Committee didn't include a single ethics specialist: All were doctors of law, medicine, biology, economics, among many other fields. Only one of the thirteen members of the committee had an advanced degree in philosophy and theology. This, to me, is telling when it comes to the type of society in which we live, one that, under the rule of economics, science and technology set the pace, while falling further and further behind to the point of becoming unreachable, is a "humanistic curiosity," one that fills the bookstore shelves with personal growth titles yet fails to resolve these sorts of issues.

Of course, when analyzing the National Bioethics Committee's makeup, what goes without saying is that everyone present should, indeed, be there, and yet not everyone who should be there is present. Even when it comes to Hippocrates, one of the fathers of medicine, technical knowledge was already intertwined with philosophical understanding. It's no coincidence that he is associated with philosophers such as Democritus and Gorgias. And when it comes to legislation, we need only to recall books like Plato's *The Laws* or Aristotle's *Politics*, two of the most well-known texts, in which philosophy is inseparable from social development and organization. But these are challenging times for philosophy, for ethical reflection (Ley Wert in Spain, and the emphasis of STEM programs over the arts in the United States), for the humanities, and above all, for critical thinking.

There's no doubt that we must promote self-inquiry and self-reflection if we're concerned about losing a philosophical approach toward life. But we must do so from within the framework of a responsible, humanistic curiosity. Being curious simply for curiosity's sake leads us nowhere. Otherwise, we might just confirm that curiosity does, in fact, kill the cat, only to genetically modify it and bring it back to life as Frankenstein's pet.

We need to foster a sense of curiosity in childhood, but if we want it to lead to practical actions, we have to outfit it with critical thinking. Curiosity is not an end in and of itself, but rather a means to achieving an objective, and we need to think in advance about the goal we want to pursue.

These are wonderful yet overwhelming times. We're constantly juggling, overextending ourselves in an effort to attend to each and every demand, or at least as many temptations as possible. This plunges us into a state of hyperactivity: Even when we're just sitting on the couch at 11:00 p.m. and trying to watch a show on TV, we can't help but also be checking the latest notifications on social media or maybe even answering a work email that just popped up in our inbox as urgent. Even when that sense of hyperactivity isn't overtly present in our lives, the emotions come flooding in: feelings of dissatisfaction, distress, and often anxiety or depression mixed with a sort of boredom that, for some people, is simply unbearable.

The shelves dedicated to personal growth books continue to expand, and there's growing interest in emotional education, not only on an academic level—just glance at the wave of new teaching strategies and training courses on emotional education being offered all over the place, as well as the increasing social demand for activities focused on controlling and/or understanding emotions: life coaching, mindfulness, meditation, yoga. There isn't a single, self-respecting gym or fitness center that doesn't offer these things as part of a "mental health" program, but is there any activity that truly addresses the healthy development of critical thinking skills? Something to help us reflect on a philosophy of life that best suits each and every individual?

We want to do things, and we want to feel good, but instead we end up anxious and stressed because when we can't do everything we want to do, we can't feel good. Immersed in the world of doing, subjected to the rule of hyperaction, it's no wonder we struggle to analyze our own life plan. Most of the time, instead of forging our own path, we end up following the paths laid out by others. Knowing what sort of guiding vision we hold—what philosophy of life is best suited to us given our circumstance—implies setting action aside and replacing it with contemplation, with reflection.

Since we're constantly living at full speed in a fast-paced world, we end up seeking hasty solutions with which to address whatever problem we've just encountered. Child psychology clinics are full, psychologists are overwhelmed, and psychiatrists' calendars are completely booked. When we turn to these "mental health professionals," we will often attend a few sessions, receive the appropriate advice or prescriptions, and expect them to take effect as quickly as possible. We're witnessing what we could now refer to as "mental health coaching" which offers specific solutions to specific problems, yet it's still unable to change an overall lifestyle. So, if we already have these support systems built into our society, why then turn to philosophy? What's the point of looking for solutions to our problems through the theories of thinkers who seem so far removed from our own lives, both in terms of historical time and social structure? The answer is quite simple: Many of the problems we're facing or will encounter did not arise spontaneously. They took time to grow, their roots spreading, and yet we try to resolve them with instant therapy. We want to quickly put a Band-Aid over the issue, but we don't follow through with an actual cure. Psychiatric and even psychological treatment are usually effective at this: In both cases, the goal is to restore balance to the problem in a given moment, but the hardest part—eradicating the root of the problem—remains. Our problems generally have a long and deeply embedded pattern of unfolding. They can't be solved in a few sessions or with a handful of pills. They require a profound reflection on the philosophy of life we've adopted, often without having realized it.

The problem with categorizing malaise as a mental illness is a relative one. What we're talking about here is more of a "philosophy of life"—to each their own—that approaches happiness in a stable, substantial way. One that will depend on each individual person and their life goals. But we certainly don't believe that most unhappy or depressed people suffer from some incurable mental illness that couldn't be addressed through good mental hygiene grounded in critical thinking. For this task, we will turn to philosophy, because philosophy is nothing more than the love of knowledge, a desire to learn and understand. Besides, it comes with more than two thousand years of experience to back it up—experience that addresses, among other things, the question of how to live a good life.

FOUR

The Grass and the Tree

This isn't the first time I've used this example, and yet I can't resist referencing it again because I believe it's a particularly illuminating metaphor in terms of understanding which mode of happiness is worth cultivating, especially when guided by critical thinking. We can choose the happiness of the grass or the happiness of the tree. Grass has many advantages. It's aesthetically pleasing. If we lie down on it, it feels soft and comfortable. It also grows quickly; we don't have to wait long before enjoying it. You plant it, you water it a little every day, and it grows. It's a very grateful little plant, yet it does have certain drawbacks that must be considered: Its roots are shallow and fragile, meaning anyone can pull it up without much effort. It needs constant care and is relatively delicate. And it suffers greatly from changes in the weather: It's the first to dry out when it doesn't receive enough water, and the first to rot under heavy, persistent rain. Finally, the ease with which it grows is matched by the ease with which it dies: The slightest event can shake its fragile structure to the core.

The tree is the complete opposite. Its seed takes a long time to germinate, and we need to wait years before we can enjoy its shade. It grows at its own pace, it's in no hurry to put the beauty of its branches and leaves on full display, focusing instead on securing a trunk and, most important, roots that allow it to face life without fear. It doesn't require much in the way of care—just a little water to get things started—but after that it's the roots that will be seeking nourishment, digging deep enough into the ground to support the rest of the trunk. Compared to grass, the tree will have no problem with changes in the weather and no fear of big storms. High winds might snap some branches or cause its leaves to fall, but with a strong foundation, the tree will remain a tree.

Once its trunk begins to strengthen, it barely needs any care at all. It's able to continue growing with little in the way of help. Once it reaches full maturity through this slow process, it can provide shade for people who gather near its trunk and shelter for other animals in its branches, allowing them to build their nests and take refuge beneath its leaves from sun and storms.

As we said in the beginning, learning to be happy—as is the case with developing critical thinking skills and maintaining good mental hygiene—takes time. But in today's society of living in the moment, speed, turbo-temporality, and instant gratification, many of us have chosen—almost without realizing it—to become grass. A plant that grows quickly, presenting an intense green exterior and a soft, pleasant texture while being exposed to all the whims of weather and human activity. Grass, though it grows quickly in order to display its viridescent blades, will still need to surround itself with more grass and other types of plants, because one lone patch does not a garden make.

I believe that our lifestyle, as well as our modes for thinking and happiness, are increasingly moving toward the grass format. People are doing what others do, they believe the notion of a joyful life is whatever those others say it is, and they need constant reinforcement from those around them. But then, when the slightest inconvenience crops up—a few drops of rain, the blazing sun on a summer day, or even a simple footstep—they experience significant suffering because neither their roots nor their stems are prepared to face adversity.

Those who grow as grass are the ones who suffer the most from the smallest details of quotidian life—the minutiae of everyday existence—because they don't know how to properly value or distinguish between the superficial and the transcendent. On the other hand, a tree won't enter into an existential crisis simply because it's raining, the wind is blowing, or someone decides to lean against its trunk, seeking shelter under its branches. Nothing less than a true catastrophe could stop the tree from continuing to grow.

In the world in which we're living, it's difficult to grow trees. Trees take time, and what we want are immediate results. But we can't forget that if we're able to achieve deeply rooted happiness, like that of the tree, we won't just experience a calming sense of security and happiness ourselves, we'll also be able to help those who come to us in search of shade, of respite, of a place to take shelter when they need it.

To this we must add an important detail: One is not happy if not fully aware of one's happiness, if it is not a deeply considered happiness developed from within. To feel is to become aware, to be able to do what, according to Socrates and the Oracle of Delphi, was the most difficult act of wisdom there is: to know oneself. A typical child who spends the day playing with friends, having fun, laughing, crying, having dinner with parents is, in the eyes of an adult, a happy child. Many would gladly trade places with that child. Just imagine, even for a moment, how wonderful it would be to return to childhood. To have no resentments, no responsibilities, nothing but innocence and the love of those who care for you.

But don't be fooled. Children are happy in the only way they can be: as children, with a childlike mindset and their own understanding of happiness. It's a happiness tailor-made for the grass: thin and fragile. They're barely able to reflect on their own sense of well-being because, again, we're talking about a very childlike sort of happiness. Indeed, it couldn't have been otherwise, for it hasn't been deliberately achieved, consciously constructed, or pondered over. The problem for many adults is that we remain anchored to this childish idea of happiness: no responsibility, easy laughter, and the ability to live in the moment without long-term life plans. But wanting to exchange our reality for the unexamined joy of infancy is a mistake, because this sort of prosperity, like grass, is fragile and insubstantial.

FIVE

Pascal and Spinoza: The Joy of Improving

"Everyone thinks" . . . such a grand and empty truth! Yes, it's true, we all think, but most people are more interested in being right than in thinking well, and that's far more troubling. Thinking has always been associated with reasoning: "Their thinking is so clear" and "Their reasoning is so clear" were and are considered synonymous. Then, intelligence was added into the mix: "They're so intelligent!" But thinking is one thing and reasoning is another. The process of reasoning is secondary with regard to thinking. From my perspective, thought is a sublime process that transcends reasoning. We can reason our way through countless situations, objectively argue millions of problems. We can rationally design an entire legal code on which we all can agree, and we can logically and methodically lay out the ideal city, just as many philosophers have throughout history. Take, for example, Plato, who, in his famous work *The Republic*, reasons about how a perfect society should be organized such that everyone benefits from everyone else. The same is true with Tommaso Campanella, with Thomas More and his *Utopia*, with Karl Marx and his communist system, and many others.

Using reason in an exemplary manner with a series of incontestable arguments does not necessarily mean that we are thinking well. In fact, when attempts were made to put some of these philosophical utopias into practice, they failed. There are many reasons for this, among which is the confusion and confounding of *reasoning* and *thinking.* We can reason—and, what's more, we might even be more right than others when it comes to objectively justifying ideas, arguments, or things—but that doesn't mean we're fully engaging in what I herein call *thinking.*

Thinking, as I see it, is an exercise that combines the two essential elements of being human: reasoning and feeling. Feeling is a fundamental part of what defines us as a species, and we cannot ignore this "humanistic side" if we truly want to learn how to think well. Thinking isn't just about activating the rational mind and objectively supplying data so that everyone reaches the same level of knowledge. It's also about understanding that data is not the whole of who we are, nor is it our purpose, and that feeling—understanding how and what it means to feel—is fundamental to knowing ourselves. This is precisely the obstacle that so-called artificial intelligence encounters when trying to mimic the human thought process.

If reasoning—that is, objectively engaging in the process of rational thought—were what truly defined us, by now we'd likely have androids much like ourselves, though with more flawless reasoning. If we were made up of nothing but pure reason, we'd be constantly exhausted, just as Pascal, another important thinker, once argued. He maintained that human beings' purpose is to think to the extent that we cannot help it; that is, thinking is in our nature, though whether we do it well is another matter entirely. Regardless, if we were to be in a constant state of thought, we'd eventually burn out, which is precisely why we need to be stirred by our passions.

Thinking also involves the subjective process—subjectivity—that unique and distinctive aspect that makes each of us who we are: singular, one-of-a-kind individuals impossible to clone. Our DNA could be replicated, of course, but to create a truly faithful replica of who we are, our memory, our experiences, our sensations would have to be transferred. Learning to think means being able to activate the two gears that work best when they are left to spin together: reasoning and feeling. We will always think from a human perspective, as José Ortega y Gasset argued, and if we want to think well, we cannot ignore this context. We can't think in a vacuum, treating ideas as if they've been completely separated from reality, affected only by the circumstance we choose through our reasoning. That's why the process of critical thinking—which we'll be exploring throughout this book—must be learned in such a way that doesn't ignore the fact that we also have feelings and emotions. These are more immediate and aren't filtered out for periods of reflection, but as we'll see in the section on decision-making, they do have a lot to contribute when it comes to thinking clearly, to thinking well.

Ever since the earliest days of philosophy, the study of emotions—how they arise, how they affect us, how to understand them, and above all, how to manage them—has been fundamental to understanding human nature. Throughout the history of human civilization, few things have changed as little as emotions. As far back as Aristotle's *Rhetoric*, we find discussions of some of the most common emotions: fear, compassion, shame, trust, intimidation, anger . . . subjects that are just as relevant to happiness as ethics and politics, both of which carry with them a significant emotional charge.

Authors such as Victoria Camps have emphasized the importance of governing our emotions as a cornerstone of ethics. In other words, learning to think means emphasizing the proper control and management of both the rational and emotional aspects of human beings.

Some philosophers have brought attention to the role of reason as an instrument of knowledge and wisdom. Others have praised the sensations and emotions for serving as the source from which all other things emanate. And then there are those who have demonstrated the importance of considering the sum of both parts. Among them, we will consider a singular thinker: Baruch Spinoza. The psychiatrist Carlos Castilla del Pino, one of the most gifted minds on the Spanish intellectual scene, and someone whom we will use as a lens through which to understand Spinoza, went so far as to say that Spinoza is the classical philosopher who most closely approaches modernity in his theory of feelings, passions, and affections.

In his book *Ethics*, Spinoza establishes a connection between emotions and reason, which he refers to as the "mind." For this thinker, emotions are closely associated with the mind's efforts to improve and, hypothetically, achieve perfection. In his understanding of the human condition, he recognizes that reason, sensation, and emotions are all sources of knowledge that work together in an inextricable way.

In Spinoza's theory, the emotion of joy arises because the mind, whether on its own or in unison with the body, has achieved a greater degree of perfection than it had before; that is, it experiences an evolution, an improvement. Joy comes from knowing that we are improving as people both physically and mentally. Conversely, pain is determined by a decline in the degree of external and internal perfection.

If we take into account this theory about the deterioration or improvement of human progress, we can accept that happiness is a way of being that can be learned. If we fail to take an active interest in this learning process, we get worse, we suffer, but if we maintain a certain amount of willpower, intelligence, and persistence in the learning process, then we will improve. For Spinoza, we progress in joy as we improve as a person, and this improvement brings us closer to perfection.

In philosophical terms, Spinoza is considered a monist. In other words, he believed that nothing existed but the body, which he understood as the place in which everything else is contained, and as such, the soul (all things related to the mind) is born, grows, and dies within it. For this particular thinker, feelings modified each person's condition. Affections alter our way of being. Thus, he wrote that "anything can be the accidental cause of joy and sorrow" (from Spinoza's *Ethics*, Part III, Proposition 15). With regard to emotions such as love and hate, he affirms:

> "If we imagine that a thing that usually affects us with the emotion of sorrow has any resemblance to an object which usually affects us equally with a great emotion of joy, we shall at the same time hate the thing and love it."

According to Spinoza, and as Castilla del Pino rightly points out, what affects us is not so much the object, not things themselves, but rather the image we have of the object. To put it another way, we create our own image of the object. The degree to which an event, idea, or issue affects us is determined not so much by what actually happens but by the way we interpret the event.

What matters is the way in which we frame and work through our thoughts, our idea that we formulate about what's happening. If we can learn to manage our critical thinking, we can reduce the power that circumstances hold over us and steel our self-control. And if we apply this to our lives to better understand ourselves, one could rightly argue that the emotions which affect us are not, in fact, caused directly by the things that are happening, but rather by the ideas we're formulating about them.

When something affects us negatively, this feeling will only be eased if we put sufficient effort into introducing something else that provokes a sense of satisfaction or happiness. Suffering can be soothed if we occupy our minds with equal yet opposite thoughts. Otherwise, reason will only intensify the pain:

> "If we hate a thing, we endeavor to affirm concerning it everything which we imagine will affect it with sorrow, and, on the other hand, to deny everything concerning it which we imagine will affect it with joy . . . We see from this how easily it may happen that a man should think too much of himself or of the beloved object, and, on the contrary, should think too little of what he hates."

In this case, reason doesn't come into play, which is why it's so important to flip the critical thinking switch as soon as possible if we want to escape from this state of hatred and sorrow. Reason can be trained to avoid falling into that declining spiral of negativity when judging something that causes us harm or pain. We mustn't forget that reason and emotion always work hand in hand, and we must pay attention to both factors when seeking to build a philosophy of life that brings us serenity and happiness.

Exercising critical thinking means learning to be better human beings because, if we listen to Spinoza, thought carries the seed of happiness. A seed that can only grow if we learn to think well and know how to use the critical thinking switch as a tool for improving ourselves through knowledge of self, for better understanding of the world around us and the circumstances in which other people's lives unfold. The simple purpose of this switch is "knowing how to be" in the universe.

"Knowing how to be" means, first of all, that we know ourselves well, that we know how to control ourselves when necessary and how to recognize the warning signs our body sends us. It means identifying our limitations, our flaws, and our strengths. In other words, it means that we know how to be at peace with ourselves. Second, yet no less important, it means knowing how to live with the circumstances surrounding us at any given moment and remain independent of the situation in which we find ourselves. Knowing how to be amid all varieties of people regardless of who they may be. Knowing we can interpret them, sense their needs, analyze their strengths, uncover their shortcomings, and, above all, we have the determination needed to act accordingly.

It's important to realize that if you use the critical thinking switch wisely, you'll not only make your life more fulfilling, authentic, and happier, but you'll also be able to improve the lives of those around you. For example, maintaining a partnership over many years—and for it to be a happy and satisfying one for both people involved—requires a high level of intelligence. The switch must be activated consistently to truly understand the other person in the relationship.

Knowing what the other person feels, empathizing or even sympathizing with them, having the foresight to anticipate what they might feel or think, opening yourself up to the other person, allowing him or her to understand who you are, developing a partnership in which both parties feel at ease, each of them allowing for independence while simultaneously appreciating the other's commitment . . . In other words, long-term relationships offer a wonderful opportunity to test our critical thinking skills and therefore see if we are truly willing to put ourselves in another person's shoes and build a happy life.

SIX

Kant: Fools and Cowards

There are many variables to consider when trying to relate critical thinking and happiness. It wouldn't be a bad idea to consider what Immanuel Kant said so eloquently in the first few lines of his essay, "An Answer to the Question: What Is Enlightenment?: "'*Sapere aude!* Have the courage to make use of your own intellect!' is hence the motto of enlightenment." Few openings are as illuminating as this short paragraph with which Kant begins his treatise on Enlightenment.

> "Enlightenment is the human being's emancipation from its self-incurred immaturity. Immaturity is the inability to make use of one's intellect without the direction of another. Tis immaturity is self-incurred when its cause does not lie in a lack of intellect, but rather in a lack of resolve and courage to make use of one's intellect without the direction of another."

But be careful . . . being an enlightened person doesn't necessarily mean knowing a lot about many things or being well-versed in a variety of subjects. Fortunately, when it comes to seeking out specific knowledge, access to specific information is right there at our fingertips, just a click away. When we talk about being enlightened, tying it to our need to grow out of our intellectual immaturity, what we're actually referring to is being an autonomous person: People who can think for themselves.

THE CHARACTER

Kant was a peculiar man who lived during the eighteenth century (1724–1804). He spent much of his life in the same city in which he was born, Königsberg, East Prussia, which at the time had a population of roughly fifty thousand inhabitants, a certain economic and commercial standing, and a university where Kant served as a professor for most of his life. His father was a saddler by trade, and his mother, as far as we know, was a German woman of great natural intelligence. They led the normal life of a Pietist family in which the mother, according to Kant himself, was kind, religious, and austere, just as this doctrine demanded.

Pietism is a branch of the Lutheran church that promotes a model of Christian life driven by piety and committed to upstanding conduct. It advocates personal, individual, and religious independence, even going so far as to declare that religion is a completely personal matter. Some scholars discern Pietist influences in Kant, drawn from the reality of his home life, which was later expressed in his philosophy, especially in the realm of morality.

It's true that philosophers have a reputation for being peculiar characters, but in Kant's case, this peculiarity is quite striking, considering we're talking about a unique person. He was austere and extremely disciplined in his habits, taking obsessive care of himself and being utterly inflexible in his routines, likely because he was in poor health. This discipline likely helped him live nearly to the age of eighty during a time when a man's average lifespan was no more than fifty. He got up every morning at 4:55 a.m. and prepared his work he had to do and the lessons he was to teach that day. He always ate surrounded by people—at least three but preferably no more than nine—because he said it was the perfect window of variation in which to enjoy a meal with company, as eating alone was considered counterproductive for health.

It's still curious that, despite holding sociability in high regard, Kant never married, never had a known partner, and expressed discomfort with the act of ejaculation, possibly due to the belief at the time that each emission meant a loss of energy. Considering how extremely careful he was with his health, it's not surprising that he made this decision and opted for celibacy. It's been said that, after eating, Kant would take the same routine walk at the same time of day to aid in digestion. But since he was rather set in his ways, he tended to walk at the same pace, speed, and intensity, following the same route to avoid breaking a sweat. He wanted to avoid any and all perspiration and had figured out exactly the right tempo he needed to maintain to avoid it, fully aware of the dangers presented by catching a chill. He was acutely meticulous about any bodily process that could lead to illness. He was both intellectual and worldly as well as being quite sociable, earning the respect of both the philosophical community of the time and the nobility. Kant rarely traveled, and yet this didn't stop him from keeping up to date with the development of such significant historical events as the American and French Revolutions. Nor did it prevent him from learning about the various philosophical, physical, and mathematical theories of the time and engaging in intellectual discussions. He hosted many gatherings at his home and enjoyed inviting prestigious individuals who specialized in differing fields of knowledge in order to stay abreast of all the latest developments.

His vast cultural knowledge (he was an avid reader), his remarkable oratory skills, and the variety and dedication he brought to his social relationships left him highly critical of those who were easily influenced by others, those who didn't subject other people's truths to their own critical judgment. His support for the Enlightenment situates him as both a prominent figure and a reference point for anyone who wants to learn to think critically, and, above all, autonomously. Kant is one of the greatest proponents of critical thinking. We need only to revisit the introductory text of his work, which I quoted earlier, to realize how important the ability to think freely and be self-reliant in life was to this man. Otherwise, we run the risk of becoming easy targets for manipulators.

COURAGE

Kant pointed out that being an enlightened person meant abandoning the intellectual immaturity in which many people take refuge throughout their lives. What did he mean by this? It's a critique of the millions who simply go along with what's happening around them—customs, habits, trends—without engaging in their own reflections on what's happening to them. *Intellectual immaturity* means assuming the thoughts and ideas of others as one's own without passing them through any sort of filter for determining whether they're truly suitable for us, whether they're right or wrong.

Being religious because that's how you were raised, being liberal or left wing because that's what you've experienced in your inner circle, getting married because that's what's expected in a stable relationship. If we broaden the spectrum of ideologies and lifestyles to the present day, we could come up with countless examples: having a social media presence because everyone else does and using it in the same way all the others do, without regard for whether it helps or harms us, wanting to make a lot of money because we've been told that's the best thing that can happen in life, traveling constantly because everyone says it's the best way to learn new things . . . In the face of all this, Kant's challenge, "*Sapere aude!*"—Dare to think!—would become the mantra of the Enlightenment.

Dare is another important word because it's easy to go with the flow, to avoid challenging ourselves, to not have to analyze or ponder the world around us. It's much easier to do what they tell you to do, to think how they say you should think, because, in doing so, we're also avoiding confrontation. But deep down we know this attitude is one of cowardice and laziness. Having someone else to always think for you is a comfortable position to be in because making decisions, especially important ones, entails a high degree of responsibility that many of us aren't prepared to assume. But if we want to construct our own philosophy of life, we have to be brave.

If we're sold on the idea of being creative, we jump into it without first analyzing whether it's beneficial to us, whether we have the necessary skills, whether it's really what best suits us, or if it's something we even enjoy. If we're told we have to be innovative, we do so. If entrepreneurship is the latest trend, we become entrepreneurs without knowing whether we have the qualities or abilities to handle it. And yet, by acting in such a way, we will never become the masters of our own lives.

We often find ourselves caught up in messy situations simply because we're doing what we're told we should be doing, and since we aren't used to analyzing our philosophy of life, nor are we in the habit of questioning other people's ideas, we let ourselves get carried away by the current. That's why I've chosen Kant as my go-to thinker when it comes to someone who can grab us by the lapels and shake us out of this slumber, shouting "Dare to think!" That's the one true way to become yourself, something that can only be achieved by developing your own philosophy of life. If you don't, you're either a sheep, a coward, or a fool.

What does it mean to be a fool?

Well, basically it means being empty-headed, not knowing how to think properly, being a simpleton, a dummy. Letting others think for you is, doubtlessly, counterproductive, because the others are not you. In other words, when you think, you do so from within yourself, through your characteristics, your context, your way of seeing and feeling things. If, all of a sudden, we allow other people to think and make decisions for us—people who don't know who we are, who are unaware of our concerns and needs—then we are simply appropriating the ideas of people who have little or nothing to do with us.

We must admit that it isn't easy to flip on what we're calling here the "critical thinking switch." In fact, it's becoming increasingly more complicated, especially in today's world. We're living during a point in history when everything around us is constantly changing and events are accelerating by the minute. And not only has the pace of life increased, but the sheer quantity of stimuli has also increased exponentially. The future has, as a temporal concept, grown closer to us, and uncertainty is now more palpable than ever. When faced with such an uncertain future, surrounded by countless contradictory and unrealistic messages, it's no wonder we don't want to hit that switch. Taking responsibility for its use can be a scary prospect. Or, to put it more directly, we've been conditioned to feel afraid. Kant is quite clear on this intimidation when he writes:

> "The guardians who have kindly assumed supervisory responsibility have ensured that the largest part of humanity (including the entirety of the fairer sex) understands progress toward maturity to be not only arduous, but also dangerous . . . It is thus difficult for any individual to work himself out of the immaturity that has become almost second nature to him. He has even become fond of it, and is, for the time being, truly unable to make use of his own reason, because he has never been allowed to try it."

We have been led to avoid thinking for ourselves. We've been kept in intellectual diapers. The "guardians" Kant speaks of are those people and institutions—social, educational, and political—that have told us it's better to follow their lead and heed their cautions. And in an even more cruel turn, Kant points to a strategy they all use to ensure none of us ever want to activate the critical thinking switch: they instill in us a fear of the consequences that might come with autonomous thought. They present it as dangerous, and when we do flip it only to inevitably fail—because we will make mistakes, over and over again—they seize upon the most insignificant misstep and use it to justify the danger and impropriety of thinking for ourselves.

They use instruments of control to impose their authority, seeking out docile, easily convinced people, especially those who don't even realize how obedient they've become. They achieve this through the subtlety of what seems to be convenient, perhaps even appropriate, under the guise of protecting humanity.

Meanwhile, they take advantage of the opportunity to plant seeds of fear deep within us.

What happens when we don't think for ourselves is that the decisions others have made on our behalf come back to haunt us. The 2014 documentary by Icíar Bollaín, titled *In a Foreign Land,* examines the consequences of Spain's economic crisis and the exodus of many young, multilingual Spaniards with college degrees who left the country for the United Kingdom, Edinburgh in particular, to earn a living in service sector jobs that didn't align with their academic training—jobs like food delivery drivers, hotel room attendants, or restaurant servers. In this documentary, some of these young people confess that they don't understand what happened to their lives because, after all, they did what they were supposed to do, what they'd been advised to do. They'd been told they had to study, graduate from college, earn a master's degree, speak multiple languages, and they did all that. But now they were finding out that none of this was of any use to them, and they felt disappointed, defrauded, and in some cases outright scammed. Can they shift the blame for the failure of their life plans to the educational system? To what extent can they absolve themselves of responsibility if they never switched on their critical thinking system? Why don't they see themselves as bearing the primary responsibility for their own decisions?

On the one hand, society has been tasked with molding obedient, docile individuals in order to make them productive for the System, but when the System realizes that the education it provides isn't adequate, it washes its hands of the matter and accuses them of not making their own decisions. In situations such as this, we can't blame just one single element. The comfort of letting ourselves get carried away on one side and the unmanageable model of production on the other are both responsible. No one took the time to teach them critical thinking skills, but these individuals also lacked the courage to question the value of the established order and maintain a philosophical attitude in the course of events.

If we want our children to mature (and this applies to ourselves as well, at any age), we need to get them accustomed to making decisions on their own from a young age, decisions that are in line with the challenges they face at their stage of life. It's a very healthy exercise in which, instead of always telling them what to do and imposing our own thoughts, we start giving them the space to make decisions for themselves. Thinking for oneself is something that can be taught, and the best way to learn it is through practice. Otherwise, we end up raising puppets: easily manipulated and controlled.

VICTIMHOOD

The feeling of victimhood professed by some of the young people in Bollaín's documentary is a symptom of not having taken control of their lives, of not having learned to switch on their critical thinking skills. The easiest, most basic thing is, as Kant says, to do what you're told to do. And, of course, when things don't turn out great after doing exactly that, that's when we start looking for someone to blame.

We firmly believe that the ones responsible for our unhappiness, our misfortune, our bad luck are always other people. The worst part is that many among us are convinced that they're the victims of their own lives—not their own executioners—and they use this mentality of victimhood as a false sense of consolation.

I'm sure we all know men and women who spend their entire lives justifying and making excuses for the bad decisions they've made without ever acknowledging that they themselves are responsible—people who don't want to think for themselves, who take refuge in the comfort of simply being obedient. They will rarely if ever achieve any profound sense of happiness because they'll always be busy looking for someone else to blame for their own poor choices. It's interesting, though, that when things are going their way, they attribute that success to listening to someone, following someone's advice, or to making the right call. To them, success lies not in the wisdom behind the advice but rather in their decision to follow it. But watch out: When the decision to follow advice or heed warnings leads to a bad outcome, the blame suddenly lies not with them—with the individuals who made the decisions—but with how bad the advice may have been or how misguided the advisor turned out to be.

On the contrary, people who make the decision to flip the critical thinking switch fully assume the risk of being right or being mistaken. They have reached a level of maturity that allows them to truly evaluate the parameters of the lifestyle they've established for themselves—they're capable of analyzing every piece of advice they've received and discarding anything that doesn't align with their personality, their way of being.

The first group consists of victims—people who always go around looking for compassion, claiming to be the martyrs of other people's bad advice, bad luck, or bad circumstances. They're incapable of recognizing the degree of responsibility they exert over their own lives. But I don't want to reduce the responsibility for the outcome of a decision to the simple act of deciding. There are always uncontrollable factors for which we can't blame anyone in particular, and yet that doesn't change the fact that the greatest burden of the decision-making process ultimately falls on oneself.

In the second group, we have more determined people, active agents in their own lives who need no reinforcement, recognition, or compassion from anyone, because they are fully aware of the responsibility they hold for their actions.

The switch works in a very particular way, because we often forget that we even have it, feeling as though we're guiding our lives properly without ever needing to engage it. In some cases, if we're not used to flipping it on, one of two things can happen: Either we get the feeling that something is wrong, but we can't figure out what it is because we can't locate the switch, or we don't know how to turn it on even after having located it. This second case represents a certain amount of progress because it assumes we at least know we have it, that we need it in order to see things more clearly, and that we're worried about not knowing how to utilize it.

Apart from foolishness or empty-headedness, what other reasons might prevent us from engaging in a healthy exercise of autonomous critical thinking? Well, Kant lays it out a paragraph later:

> "Idleness and cowardice are reasons why such a large segment of humankind, even after nature has long since set it free from foreign direction (*naturaliter maiorennes*), is nonetheless content to remain immature for life; and these are also the reasons why it is so easy for others to set themselves up as their guardians. It is so comfortable to be immature. If I have a book that reasons for me, a pastor who acts as my conscience, a physician who determines my diet for me, etc., then I need not make any effort myself. It is not necessary that I think if I can just pay; others will take such irksome business upon themselves for me."

Little could be added to a beautiful and sensible argument. If I can pay, I don't need to think. But money, if not used wisely, brings more dissatisfaction than joy.

In 2014, Michael Norton and Elizabeth Dunn published *Happy Money: The Science of Happier Spending* based on the results of their studies on the relationship between money and happiness. They present a high percentage of people whose lives, after winning large sums of money in a lottery, became even more miserable than they were before. They thought the money would buy them a good life, but they were wrong. As soon as they collected their winnings, they moved into upper-class neighborhoods or relocated to other cities. They enrolled their children in private schools, bought villas or remote, isolated houses, and changed their routines and habits. All this happened overnight, without a transitionary period, because they believed they now had to live in such a way that corresponded to their economic status. The consequences were catastrophic. They broke ties with the social circle they used to live in, uprooted their children from their familiar environs, traded in their previous social model for one they weren't accustomed to, and eventually felt even more miserable than they were before becoming rich. Friends and family members asked them for money, and they became distrustful of every new person they met, unsure whether that person was interested in them or their money.

Among Norton and Dunn's conclusions, one in particular stands out: Money can bring happiness, but only if we know how and—above all—with whom to spend it. According to their data analysis, money significantly increases happiness if it is spent and shared with others rather than wasting it on oneself. Many of the newly rich thought that money was the best guardian for their lives, but they were wrong: They didn't use the critical thinking switch.

There are times in life when having an advisor—a guide, someone who offers the perspective of experience—is always a positive. Society takes care of these details when we're young and know almost nothing about either ourselves or the world around us. This is why, when we're children, it's just as important for guardians (parents, teachers, and in some cases religious figures) to offer guidance on things we should be doing as it is for them to present us with options and give us the freedom—and the accountability that comes with it—to make the decision. A good guardian will push us to make these choices for ourselves. But problems arise when we, as adults, still need these guardians to tell us how to navigate our lives, and when we simply accept their instructions without any prior review or reflection. At that point, no matter how old we may be, we're immersed in the intellectual immaturity to which Kant refers. In the twenty-first century, it seems as though comfort is the standard-bearer of happiness. If we want to do a good job when it comes to education—or educating ourselves—we have to give up the comforts that lie in not making decisions, not conducting any analysis.

One of the keys to a person's success is being able to do two things vital for achieving well-being: making decisions independently and taking responsibility for the consequences of those decisions.

The banner we most proudly wave here in the twenty-first century—one that has become embedded in any way of life worthy of respect, is that of freedom. We proclaim and defend our right to be free. Freedom is untouchable, the object of greatest desire to those who do not possess it. But while we consider freedom to be nonnegotiable, we fail to educate ourselves on its proper use, and we fail to teach others about the consequences of access to said freedom.

One of society's most pressing challenges for a person in learning to think and build one's own philosophy of life involves a true understanding of what freedom entails. An understanding of how to take proper advantage of it, to appreciate its depth, its weight. Ideally, within an educational setting, we would grant certain freedoms, almost as a mandate, so that people must face the challenges presented by freedom. We would grant it to them in small portions so they're aware of what happens as it becomes part of their lives. These doses would gradually increase until they reach intellectual maturity.

Maturity means not depending on anyone when it comes to making decisions about your own life. It also means taking responsibility for them. Being educated on the nature of freedom at a young age is necessary if people are to confront it later. When children are in elementary school, they are offered little in the way of choice when it comes to books, subjects, classmates—everything has been predetermined by professionals who believe they know what's best for children. And yet, as they grow, the educational system itself begins to offer a set of options from which children must choose, a decision they are often unprepared for because they have yet to face the full weight of freedom.

When young students finish middle school or junior high, they are forced to choose between a number of options: drop out, enroll in a vocational-technical program, or earn a high school diploma. If they opt for the vo-tech or high school route, they will be forced to select from a wide range of programs and specializations, choices that will later shape their collegiate studies or professional careers. In many cases, it's the parents of these students who make the decisions for them, driven by the best of intentions along with the conviction that they're doing what's best for their children. However, in these cases, they're actually preventing their children from learning one of life's most important lessons: the value of freedom. These are the moments when the child, the student, the son or daughter must come face-to-face with the imposition of freedom. Freedom requires them to make choices, to make decisions they know could be crucial to their future. Such circumstances can be difficult for some, unpleasant for others, and tense and stressful for almost all because they're at an age when they scarcely need to confront freedom in any real way at all. Until this point, most decisions have been made on their behalf by others, and life itself has been rather uncomplicated.

Many of us would rather not have to make decisions, to not face freedom so alone, to not be forced to deal with this model of decision-making in which we and we alone, for the most part, will be responsible for what happens afterward. But when we do, we increase our degree of autonomy and foster growth in our critical thinking skill set. In these situations, it's not just about choosing comfort over decision making as a way of life. We're talking about something more problematic when it comes to progress: cowardice.

This isn't the first time, nor will it be the last, that fear overwhelms us, paralyzing us when we're faced with a decision that rests solely upon our shoulders. We don't have the courage to face the situation; we'd pay to keep things the way they were, without having to confront anything, without having to feel responsible for our future (getting married, having children, taking out a mortgage, getting divorced). That's why Kant ends the second paragraph we've read with one of the most famous mantras in human history: *Sapere aude!*—Dare to think!—a phrase that emphasizes two very significant actions for anyone who wants to take life by the reins. On the one side, as we've already discussed, there's bravery, boldness, the courage to be the one who decides what to do without the need for guidance. On the other, there's the act of thinking critically in order to set in motion a life filled with wonderful challenges and moments that you'll truly treasure because the joys of uncovering them will be yours.

SEVEN

Socrates: Good People

Another key issue when it comes to learning how to be happy—one we don't always know quite how to deal with—is related to our conscience: that little voice that sometimes keeps us awake at night, nagging us when we haven't done things the way we should have. How can we be happy if we feel bad about ourselves, if we have that infamous guilty conscience? To prevent this from happening, we have to learn to act morally, to be what's known in popular slang as "good people." Bad people can never be happy. As the saying goes, "The thief sees everyone else as a thief," and they're right. To be happy, we must be good people who don't harm others or wish harm upon anyone. We can't confuse revenge's satisfaction with happiness because, among other reasons, revenge affects another person while happiness is exclusive to oneself, something personal.

To avoid feeling bad, we need to learn how to think well. A guilty conscience arises either because we haven't considered the consequences of our actions before committing them (which ends up harming someone else) or because, even if we were clear about what those consequences would be, we haven't foreseen how the outcome would affect us. Socrates had an interesting theory on this subject. He argued that a guilty conscience was synonymous with stupidity, with foolishness. To Socrates, people who harmed others did so because they were fools. People act wrongly out of ignorance.

For this Greek thinker, evil was a direct consequence of ignorance. Evil people were simply ignorant, but of what? Of the consequences of their actions; that is, they hadn't properly taken into account the pain, the harm they were going to inflict on others or even themselves. If they had been clear from the start about what they wanted to achieve and then achieved it, then they were ignorant of the consequences of those actions. In other words, they didn't have the requisite knowledge of self to be able to bear the consequences of their own wrongdoings.

In Socrates's way of thinking, which is known as "moral intellectualism" and which boils down to saying those who act wrongly do so because they are idiots, because they can't grasp the fact that the ones who will ultimately suffer the most harm, whether directly or indirectly, will be themselves.

Some accuse him of being naïve and simplistic in his approach to life. But for us, it's very important to highlight the need to switch on our critical thinking skills before taking action in order to avoid the suffering that often accompanies the consequences of those actions. But is that really being naïve? Isn't it the case that people who commit evil acts end up unhappier than before even when they achieve their goals? Don't they end up isolated? Causing harm to another person will bring you anything but happiness. Sadism and vengeance, two behaviors focused on hurting others, can provide momentary pleasure and satisfaction, but again, we cannot confuse these feelings with happiness. If choosing a lifestyle based upon harming others is a conscious choice, then isn't that the choice of an unintelligent person? Perhaps Socrates wasn't quite so naïve after all.

Another philosopher who can help us analyze our behavior is, again, Kant, who spent a lot of time thinking about how to distinguish a good action from a bad one. That is, he wanted to answer the question of how we should act throughout our lives in a world where we have to coexist and interact with others. He became obsessed with finding a universal ethic, a way of conducting ourselves that would work for all while also being quite simple, lacking in any great complications. He wrote a book titled *Groundwork of the Metaphysics of Morals* (as you can see, Kant wasn't very good at coming up with catchy, popular titles), and while his books are dense, profound philosophical works with a specialized audience (which is normal, considering the period we're talking about, when only a privileged few had access to a college education), the conclusions he reaches can be absorbed and understood by anyone without needing to be a scholar.

What can we take from Kant's ethics in terms of our goal of learning to think well? Primarily, it's that, in the course of our daily lives, we should act in a moral manner. Can there be one single ethic in which we all agree on how to define a moral action, a good action? Kant thought so. What sort of good behavior could become universal? As we've already seen, Kant's hope was that people think for themselves.

We must rid ourselves of the doctrines that tell us how we should behave. These doctrines, which we accept without any preceding analysis, were of no interest to the German philosopher because, in the end, there's very little of you in everything you do, and a lot of doing what you're told to do. It's as if you're carrying around an instruction manual on how to conduct yourself written by someone who doesn't know you, who doesn't have anything at all to do with you, and yet you accept it as your own without ever having flipped the critical thinking switch. With that in mind, let's take a moment to think about ourselves. Can we truly consider ourselves good people if we're simply following some external code of conduct?

If we always do what we've been told is right, then what merit is there in being good people? The only one we would have (if it can be considered a merit at all) is that of being obedient, to which Kant would say that a good action is one that can only be guided by good will. In other words, when we're about to do something, Kant advises us to think first about whether we would want someone else, in the same situation, to do what we're about to do. To determine if an action is good, we have to look at the intent behind what we're doing rather than the consequences. The only thing we can control—the one thing we can be completely certain of—is the goodwill we put into what we're doing. But once we've done something, once the action has been set in motion, it is no longer ours. Instead, it belongs to unforeseeable factors beyond our control.

If we want to know whether we're good people, we have to think before we act, and this manner of thinking, which Kant called the "Categorical Imperative," will tell us whether we're acting rightly or wrongly. It's truly quite simple: When you're about to do something, think about whether you would want everyone in your situation to do the same. If your answer is "Yes, I would expect anyone in my situation to do what I'm about to do," then the action would be a good one because the will behind it is one you intend to be a universal one. You wouldn't mind if your partner, your children, your friends, or your parents did the same. But if the answer is "No," then you can be quite certain that you're not acting in good conscience.

This way of acting helps us improve our self-esteem, allowing us to perceive ourselves as a good person, as someone who knows that what one is doing is right, someone who can sleep with a clear conscience because the decision was one's own and would love for everyone to do the same. This doesn't mean we completely discard the way we've been acting until now. We've probably all done what we've been told is right at one time or another, and much of that behavior was guided by external agents: religion, school, the media, existing laws . . . Elements that indoctrinate us, that orient us so we know how to behave in what's supposed to be the most appropriate way when it comes to living in a community, in a society made up of all sorts of people with different perspectives on life and behavior. The key is to review these actionable processes and make them our own, turn them into our own personal ways of proceeding forward, and after having analyzed and filtered through them, we will likely find that many of them are reasonable enough to put into practice.

EIGHT

Daniel Bernoulli: How to Make Good Decisions

Being able to flip the critical thinking switch isn't something that happens overnight. Each and every day, as soon as we wake up in the morning, we are forced to face one of the most important processes when it comes to shaping your personality: decision making. Throughout your life, you'll face all kinds of decisions: decisions about work that can affect you or your colleagues, decisions about love, health, the economy . . . and we'd all like to be making the correct decisions, but how can such a thing be achievable? Harvard Professor Dan Gilbert can lend some insight into decision theory, citing an eighteenth-century scientist (mathematician, physicist, physician, etc.) by the name of Daniel Bernoulli. Of the many studies conducted on decision theory, I'd like to highlight an equation Bernoulli proposed as an attempt to explain how one can make the right decisions. We can summarize this equation as follows:

> "The value that we expect from any action we are going to perform, from any decision we are going to make (that is, the good we expect from them), is the result of two things:

first, the probability we assign to the likelihood that this decision or action will allow us to gain something, and secondly, the value that this action/decision holds for us."

According to Bernoulli, if we know whether a decision will benefit us in any way and are also aware of the value and real benefit it will entail for us, then we will always be able to calculate which decision/action to take, because we will correctly know what we will gain from it and what value we will assign to that gain.

But, as Professor Gilbert rightly points out, the problem lies in the fact that, in everyday life, we can be quite clumsy, unaware, or overly optimistic or pessimistic when it comes to estimating the value of the benefit we might receive. We're extremely obtuse when it comes to evaluating the first factor: the probability of success we assign to the decision we are about to make. And we're not very good at assessing the second factor either: the value that the outcome of those decisions holds for us.

If we focus on the first factor—the probability of success we assign to a decision—the data shows us that we're actually quite terrible at calculating those probabilities. In most cases, we're all but completely unaware of the actual odds of success when making a choice, and the lottery is an excellent example of this. We play the lottery because we refuse to acknowledge the extremely low (nearly zero) chance of winning. It's almost like throwing money away, and yet we keep trying because we're unable to calculate the actual odds of winning . . . or, rather, we don't want to stop and think about it. So, given this, why do we keep playing La Primitiva in Spain and Mega Millions or Powerball in the United States? There are a number of reasons. One is because we often see that there is, indeed, a winner (just watch the news the day after the Christmas lottery draw). Who isn't sitting there holding a ticket? The fact of the matter is that the losers, the gambling addicts, or those who play the same numbers week in and week out without ever winning anything in their entire lives are never the headlines. As such, the lone image of the lucky winner overrides rational calculations.

Gilbert offers us a very simple example of how our brain operates when making a decision about calculating the probabilities of success. Imagine that, at a parent-teacher conference, I want to hold a raffle for a weekend at a five-star hotel in Barcelona. I have ten €20 tickets. Nine different families have already bought their tickets and are asking if you want one. Normally you'd buy in because the odds aren't bad: Everyone in the room has a one-in-ten chance of winning, and since each family has one ticket, we decide to grab the last one left. Now, imagine that just one single family has bought nine of the ten tickets, and that you're being encouraged to take the remaining one. All of a sudden, your feelings change, because you gather that this one family is almost certain to win. The problem is that you feel your odds of winning in this second case are much lower, whereas in reality you have the exact same probability of winning in both examples. You just don't perceive it as such, because the second part of the equation—the part that estimates the value we place on the outcome of a decision—is much more complex.

Trying to determine how much something is worth, how much we'll enjoy it, or even how much pleasure and satisfaction it will bring us is extremely difficult if we don't turn on our critical thinking switch. This tends to happen because, in many cases, when we estimate the value of something before we've actually owned or enjoyed it, we do so by comparing it to our past, to what we've experienced previously. And, in doing so, we forget something very important: present context.

Let's look at another example to help us better understand how we make decisions. Imagine you want to take a Mediterranean cruise, and when you visit the cruise website, you see an offer that says a package originally priced at €2,000 has just been reduced to €1,400. Normally, you'd snap it up and feel very satisfied with your purchase. But now picture another example: You visit the website and see the package is on sale for €700, but when you call the travel agency, you're told the offer has expired and the cruise will cost you €1,400, which is still a significant discount from the original €2,000. In this second case, you're a lot less likely to make the purchase. Your mind is set on the fact that the price is much higher than it was just a few days ago. That reference to the past has subjectivized the price. What we're doing is what we so often do when calculating value: We situate ourselves in the past, anchored to a different price we've seen before. In other words, when calculating the value something will have for us in the future, we tend to be guided by our previous experiences, which is only logical. But it's also why, when it comes to making decisions, especially those related to the most important aspects of life—comparing one love against another, the apartment you previously had with the one you're living in now, the education you received versus the one you're getting now—we don't always get it right. Still, it seems as though comparison is unavoidable when it comes to figuring out the value we will assign to something.

What we need to bear in mind is that, when assessing something, comparisons change its perceived worth. We must be aware that if we assign a specific value to a decision or an object before we have it, the most appropriate thing to do would be to avoid comparing it with anything else, because doing so will alter our assessment. It could make it seem more or less valuable, more or less prestigious Either way, we are stripping it of the original value we had planned to assign it long before making the actual purchase.

We're not always honest or reasonable when it comes to assigning not just a value to something but the value it truly ought to have. If, for example, I want to buy a laptop and the store near my home is asking for €400, but a shop in a small town nine miles from the city is asking for €300, then I'll go buy it there because that seems like a significant savings. But if I want to buy a car and the dealership near my house is asking for €15,100 while one in the same nearby town is priced at €15,000, then many will decide to skip the trip and pay the extra €100 for the convenience of buying it close to home. In both cases, however, we're talking about the exact same difference of just €100. When it comes to the computer, it seems like an incredibly important savings, but with regards to the car, we don't lend it nearly any importance at all. The most curious part of all this is that, in both cases, our financial situation is the same: Our savings and income levels haven't changed. In the former case, saving seems like common sense—an almost ethical obligation—because not doing so would leave us feeling like we're wasting money, yet in the latter situation, we're at peace with spending a little extra because, in the context of such high figures, the amount seems all but insignificant. This is just one more example of how irrationally we can act when it comes to estimating the value of something.

If we want to develop our critical thinking skills properly, we need to stay away from comparisons and focus strictly on the intrinsic value itself, regardless of the context in which it appears.—whether it's a laptop or a car, €100 is €100, and we can't add or subtract value depending on what we're referring to.

In short, to protect ourselves psychologically, we've chosen to do two things completely contrary to Bernoulli's advice:

Downplay our probability of suffering future harm or pain (which is precisely why we don't take issues from climate change to junk food to overpopulation seriously on a personal level; instead, we underestimate the very real possibility that these problems can and will have a direct affect upon us) while at the same time overvaluing immediate gratification, embracing a carpe diem mindset as if there were no future at all. Ultimately, of course, we end up suffering the consequences of the poor decisions we make.

NINE

Barry Schwartz: The Burden of Having to Choose

Let's use some practical cases to put critical thinking to work for everyday personal situations. Life is an adventure that must be lived for oneself; otherwise, it will end up being a miserable, impoverished life because it was lived through someone else's eyes. And for us to be the protagonists of our own story, we must "dare to think" and make decisions. When Kant proposed the *sapere aude!* mantra, it was with the Age of Enlightenment in mind and a civil paradigm to be claimed: freedom. To make choices, one must have freedom. But freedom would be meaningless if there were no options from which to select. These two parameters—freedom and options from which to choose—are essential for any person's development.

To analyze the importance of decision making under the umbrella of critical thinking, we will look to Professor Barry Schwartz, author of a book titled *The Paradox of Choice: Why More Is Less*. If daring to think is our goal, the obstacles in our way can best be overcome through decision making.

There's a sort of common ideology in which we think that freedom is always a good thing, that the more freedom we have, the better. But for freedom to exist, there must also be alternatives from which to choose; otherwise, it would be all but impossible to "choose" something when there is only one possible option. To put it another way, if there's only one political party to vote for, the sense of freedom is obviously meaningless. What Professor Schwartz has demonstrated through experiments is that there's a dangerous correlation between increased freedom and the increased options associated with freedom. We tend to assume that more options signify more freedom. To a certain extent, this holds true. But when these options become so plentiful as to become overwhelming, then problems arise that prevent us from making decisions. Still, people tend to prefer to have as many options as possible, believing that the more choices they have, the greater their sense of freedom will be.

Think about it: What actually happens when we're faced with a multitude of options while trying to make a decision? The answer is simple: We freeze up, we become anxious, overwhelmed, feeling saturated with choices and overwhelmed by the situation. And this is precisely where we need to flip on our critical thinking skills.

In a hyperstimulated, hyper-diverse, multi-optional world in which we feel as though we can have it all, it's essential to engage our critical thinking systems to remain happy and avoid feeling distressed in situations that should actually be favorable to us because we have many options and the freedom to choose from among them. When it comes to children, especially when they're young, they face countless situations in which the multitude of options could cause unnecessary anxiety . . . selecting one video game from among the dozens that are available, for example. They could well be racked with doubt because they'd like to try them all out first and be sure they're selecting the one that will entertain them the most. The same goes for writing letters to Santa. In this particular case, I've witnessed firsthand a phenomenon that has become normalized in many families when it comes to which toy their child truly wants for Christmas. I'm talking parents and children jointly reviewing toy catalogs. When these glossy magazine-like ads arrive, parents either sit down and flip through them with their kids or simply hand them over. The children are drawn to so many different toys, most of which have no connection or tie-in to any other, and soon enough they want them all. Parents then set a limit, either in the form of a quantity (you can choose three or four) or an amount (no more than €100), which almost immediately sets in motion a process of dissatisfaction and frustration, because the children already know they have to choose between many things they want while giving up others. And while we might believe that having to choose from multiple options—that is, being forced to make a decision—is a positive exercise in maturity, the lessons learned from such an activity aren't always suitable for their personal development.

The more appropriate thing to do, long before showing them the catalog, which will only serve as an instantaneous influence, would be for children to learn to define their preferences and identify the types of games they feel most comfortable with, the ones they will enjoy the most. Neither the catalog (and, by catalog, we're obviously including TV commercials) nor the toys should trigger a need or desire. Before seeing any of these things, it's far more instructive to conduct a simple exercise in which children reflect on the toys and games they already have, the ones they use the most, the ones they like best . . . in other words, children should be able to participate in a simple yet effective and honest act of introspection about how they tend to play. To think about whether they prefer solitary, more imaginative play, whether they'd rather play in groups of friends, siblings, neighbors, or family members, whether they're into technology or building kits like Legos. Whatever the case may be, the idea is that—before external desires and cravings take hold—we are able to flip on the critical thinking switch and help them make their own thoughtful choices.

It's not all that complicated. We just have to know how to read the moment. If we train ourselves to do this, the circumstances themselves will let us know when it's time to engage our critical thinking skills. We just need to learn how to decode these signals we're receiving, both externally and from within ourselves. We must teach people that, when they find themselves in a situation in which having to make a choice feels overwhelming and stressful, they can center themselves and begin by analyzing their particular needs, shortcomings, and wishes. When we don't know what to do, when we've fallen into an emotional slump or feel paralyzed with anxiety, we start to feel empty or insecure, and we're not quite sure how to navigate our lives under the weight of important decisions that must be made. And those moments are precisely when flipping the critical thinking switch is most important.

When it comes to making simple, everyday choices, the results usually aren't very problematic, at least initially. Issues arise when the availability of choices and the freedom to choose are vast. This combination—a breadth of choices with an abundance of freedom—is often the starting point for stressful situations, and when the sum of these situations reaches a certain point, anxiety and a constant sense of dissatisfaction with the life we're leading begin to take root.

Let's look at a few examples to better understand this situation . . . and since I'm foolish enough, I'll start by offering my own. Not long ago, I decided to swap out my television for a new one. We'd had the same, regular, 32-inch TV for twelve years. Nothing fancy, but it worked just fine. It wasn't HD, but the images were good, or so I thought, until one day I walked into someone's house, looked at their TV, and was struck by the difference in picture quality. My family has never been too picky when it comes to electronics. The problem with that, though, started three years ago when someone gave us some documentaries on a flash drive, and we realized there was no way for us to plug it in. We couldn't even connect our computer. And to top it all off, when our son got a video game console as a gift, the TV didn't have an HDMI cable input, and we had to plug it in to the computer monitor instead.

After several years of browsing the electronics section in various shopping malls without ever buying one—after all, ours wasn't broken, so there was no pressing need to replace it—we finally decided it was time to buy a more modern unit. So, I started looking at makes and models, which is where the trouble began: screen size, image resolution, processing speed for internet connectivity, weight, auxiliary ports. Since I hadn't flipped on my critical thinking switch, I decided to do some research on the internet and even joined an online forum to see if anyone could offer me some advice. Big mistake! Everybody had an opinion regarding the perfect TV: the pros and cons of certain brands, the most common issues, the best stores from which to buy them. Within a forty-eight-hour span, I'd come to realize that every TV within our budget seemed to come with a "but": some flaw, some drawback, some problem. And let me pause here to point to something you may have glossed over: forty-eight hours. I'd spend no less than two full days comparing prices and deals online, and I'd visited all four electronics stores in my city. That's when I hit a wall. Worn out, uncertain, and disinclined to buy anything at all, I decided it was finally time to hit the switch and start thinking critically. I asked myself,

"How is it even possible that I've spent all my free time studying and researching TVs, and yet now I'm having more trouble than ever picking one?" I place part of the blame on two factors that are actually secondary in nature: the overwhelming amount of information on any topic, and the ease with which one can access that information, whether it's verified or not. But I also blame my own foolishness for not having flipped on my critical thinking switch sooner.

At that same moment, I realized what I was searching for was the perfect TV. I wanted to make the perfect choice without a single, lingering regret. I wanted everyone who knew about televisions and who happened to see the one I bought to tell me I'd come to the right decision. But most of all, I wanted to make sure I wasn't making a mistake. So, I did something very simple in order to not spend any more time on such a trivial matter, which I wasn't enjoying in the least. I went to one of the stores I'd visited, told the sales associate my needs and my budget, and asked for a recommendation. It wasn't until that moment that I realized it was easier to identify my desires (as well as my needs) and search based on those parameters rather than attempt to make a selection based on existing options.

When I flipped the switch, what I wanted was all quite clear to me: an HDTV between forty and fifty inches in size, the latest model possible, one that could read a variety of flash drive formats and project both audio and video when connected to a computer, all that within a very specific price range. Nothing major to be asking for. I didn't care much about the brand, the aesthetics, the online services that came with it, or any of the countless features and options that the labels claimed it had. The sales associate, who recognized me from having come in twice in the past three days, quickly sensed my frustration and fatigue. He suggested two models within €30 of each other.

Since I didn't feel like making choices of any kind by that point, I left the decision up to him. In other words, a salesperson, who's a professional in the field, chose the television I now have in my home. When we turned it on for the first time, it felt like a miracle: All the *a posteriori* requirements I'd set had been met, and my anxiety, anger, and exhaustion had been lifted off my shoulders.

But the story doesn't end there. Over the years, I've also learned that once I make a choice among many similar options, I stop thinking about the ones I passed over and instead focus on convincing myself that I make the right decision. The TV I now have at home is the one I'd always wanted; I just didn't realize it until I flipped my critical thinking switch. Since then, I've always tried to apply this decision-making methodology when it comes to things I don't know much about and that appeal to me even less. I'd identify what I needed or wanted and then go look for options that met those requirements. The key is to not set the bar too high, and most of all, to be clear about what you really need and want.

THE ART OF SATISFACTION

Proper thinking means changing the dynamics of choice. Barry Schwartz has described two types of people based on the way they approach the decision-making process. I've analyzed this topic on more than a couple occasions, and yet I never get tired of repeating it. On the one hand, there are those whom we might call "Maximizers," people who always want to make the perfect choice, to get the most out of the decisions they make. They study all the options, analyze them from every angle, and dedicate all available time to reading all the information they can get their hands on in order to understand every last detail before making a decision. These people are destined to suffer because, in a world like ours, the options are so vast, so varied, so titanic in nature that there will always be some element of their decision they're not completely happy about, leading them to agonize during the decision-making process and, even worse, after the fact. These are people who, once they've made a decision, instead of disconnecting and taking a deep breath of relief to confirm their choice, are still often interested in seeing other options. Later on, when they uncover something that's better than what they have, they regret not having waited just a bit longer to grab it up. These are people who generally don't activate their critical thinking skills, instead allowing themselves to be carried away by anxiety and the pressure of not being able to make any mistakes.

On the other side of the scale are the "Satisficers," people who, when confronted with a choice, choose not to complicate their lives in the least. They know what they want, what they need, they have it clearly defined so that all that's left is to pick something that satisfies those conditions. They're not always looking for the best, they're not out to make the perfect purchase at the perfect time. On the contrary, they tend to be pleased or at least satisfied with their choices because they know from the start what they need or want, thus making the goal more easily achieved as well as more gratifying. Maximizers dismiss Satisficers as complacent, as people who simply settle, as if being content with choosing something that suits their needs were some sort of unfortunate condition. And Satisficers label Maximizers as perfectionists who can never accept the choices they've made. Just stop and think for a moment: Which of the two do you think is actually happier?

The problem lies not only in the decision-making model we must adopt, but also in the advertising methodology employed by consumerism that can turn us, whether we're aware of it or not, into Maximizers. We are constantly bombarded with offers to the point where some companies even imply that Satisficers aren't intelligent consumers: "We're not stupid," they say, emphasizing the social importance of smart shopping. In fact, more and more, in everyday conversations, people are publicly boasting about finding the best restaurant in the city, knowing where to buy the freshest fish, being able to recommend the best hotel to stay in if you're visiting Venice, or where the high-end clothes are on sale for half off. Presenting oneself in society as an intelligent consumer is held in high regard. It has become something of a hallmark that one should always be proud of because it associates seemingly divergent concepts: consumption and intelligence. That's why everyone wants to boast that they always make the best choices because they're the most intelligent of consumers.

But this problem is compounded by a more profound one. The issue of material consumption becomes even more serious if we extrapolate this consumerist methodology to other aspects of our life, such as work, love, or raising children. In other words, when the human factor has to decide how to handle deeper emotions on top of dealing with modern life, we end up physically and mentally exhausted.

When it comes to making choices that are deeply important to us and our lives, or when we're faced with situations or choices that might also affect other people, critical thinking must be guided by the most emotional of decisions, provided that the rational part has concluded that the options before us are relatively equal. When needs are identified, and we know more or less what we want, and if we have multiple options that each at least partially offer what we're looking for—each with positive and negative aspects that we examine with the same scrutiny—then (to use a common expression) we have followed our heart. In the case where there is relative equality among options, it would be advisable to choose the one to which we feel the strongest emotional attachment.

It's very important, when making major decisions that can radically affect our lives, like deciding whether our partner is truly the right one for us, or whether he or she is the best person to start a family with, that we avoid taking on the Maximizer role. It's absolutely essential to not cling to the notion of making the absolute best choice from among all possible options, because when it comes to emotional matters, there's simply no guarantee. Learning to be an emotional Satisficer helps us to recognize that our emotional needs are being met and to understand that we can't expect the other person to be perfect or perfectly fulfill each and every one of our expectations.

Let's look at another basic example: buying a property with the goal of turning it into a home. Rationally, we want a four-bedroom apartment because we have two children and also like the idea of converting one room into an office with a desk and bookshelves. But all the four-bedroom apartments we've inspected seem to be missing something. They're all decent places, they're within our budget, and they're located in nice neighborhoods, but after having taken the tour, we leave without feeling entirely convinced. Suddenly, one day, the real estate agent whose been guiding us through the hunt calls and insists that we check out a three-bedroom unit because they've got a feeling we'll love it.

As soon as we walk in, we immediately fall in love with it: the bathrooms, the living room, the kitchen, the views—everything is spectacularly decorated, and we leave feeling completely charmed by the place, though with a twinge of hesitation because it only has three bedrooms. Well, according to the decision-making model we've been discussing, if we want to make the right decision, we have to follow our hearts and make an offer on the three-bedroom apartment. And you'll see why: If we opt for one of the four-bedroom apartments we've seen, then every day we walk through that door, we'll have to convince ourselves that this was what we were looking for, that it met the needs we established for ourselves, and that this litany of internal justification will help us feel at peace with our choice. We'd have to constantly remind ourselves that we made the best, most rational decision. However, if we buy the three-bedroom apartment, every day when we get home, we'll say and feel that our home is lovely. In time, we'll find a spot for our books, we'll create a space to set up our desk and computer. In other words, the emotions we felt the first time we walked through that door will still be alive every morning we wake up in that three-bedroom apartment. Eventually, we'll find ways to adjust some of our original requirements so we can continue enjoying that wonderful feeling.

The same set of criteria should be followed when, to cite another example, we have to choose between one job and another, both of which have advantages and disadvantages. In this case, it's always advisable to go with the job that appeals to you the most, even if it means having fewer financial incentives or less vacation time. When we're facing major decisions—major choices that will have a profound effect on our lives—and utilizing rational criteria still leaves us unsure, then we must listen to the emotional component because that's what will give us the daily energy to feel good about the decision we ultimately make.

TEN

Lipovetsky: The Value of Contradiction

One of the biggest problems we encounter in our everyday lives is that we always want to be right. We want to know that we're right and to impose that authenticity on every idea, argument, or opinion that comes our way. But occasionally we'll try to win a debate not because we truly believe we're correct but because we want to assert rhetorical superiority over the other person, to come up with a better argument against them even though we know deep down that we don't actually agree with what we're saying. There are plenty of occasions in which being right and shutting down a discussion has nothing to do with uncovering the truth.

The search for truth has always been the quintessential goal of philosophy and, by extension, humanity itself. Finding it, however, is a different story. And while the aim of this book isn't to discover the truth or analyze what may or may not be true, we are committed to trying to better understand who we truly are. We must strive to better understand this world—a world we are reshaping at a breakneck pace—and then, with that understanding, put our critical thinking machinery to work.

This is no small matter, which is why it's important for us to accept that we are human beings and not robots. It's also why it's so difficult for the much-hyped "Artificial Intelligence" to be like us, to think like us, or to act like us. Despite scientific advances in understanding human beings, we still don't know how a thought is formed, how a so-called irrational decision is made, or how all the contributing factors come into play, simply because no matter how hard we try, every human being is unique in their history, their experiences, their knowledge, in how they feel, in their tolerance for pain, and, of course, in their way of thinking.

There are many factors that influence our patterns of thought, and some philosophers have concluded that we can, at times, be contradictory, that we can act against the dictates of logic. Or, as Gilles Lipovetsky asserts, that we are paradoxical. Distinguished philosophers such as Michel de Montaigne acknowledged a certain contradiction within their own ideas, even their own lives, and this is reflected in their work. It's advisable to recall a few words from his *Essays*:

> "We are, I know not how, double in ourselves, so that what we believe we disbelieve, and cannot rid ourselves of what we condemn . . . We float between different states of mind; we wish nothing freely, nothing absolutely, nothing constantly."

When it came to describing himself, Montaigne went so far as to say:

> "Bashful, insolent; chaste, lustful; prating, silent; laborious, delicate; ingenious, heavy; melancholic, pleasant; lying, true; knowing, ignorant; liberal, covetous, and prodigal."

As Professor Manuel Bermúdez has rightly pointed out, much of Montaigne's work focuses on knowledge of self as a path toward living a good life. In this regard, Montaigne was clear that Fortune did not play an essential role in the pursuit of this grand task. In fact, the French thinker was not a determinist; that is, he did not believe in predetermined events. As such, we are obliged to struggle with the internal contradictions that confront us daily if we are ever to achieve that goal: learning to lead a good life.

We must learn to accept the value of contradiction in our lives as something natural and intrinsic to the human condition. Otherwise, we will become an unhappy species, unable to accept our own contradictions or those of others. But when we refer to "contradiction," we do so from the perspective of a paradox. We are paradoxical beings; we want to exist in a certain way, we idolize people who have achieved a certain standard of living or who present a way of being we consider admirable. But when the time comes, we make no real effort to imitate them, to become more like these role models. Occasionally we're able to develop the most impeccable reasoning from a logical standpoint and understand perfectly well what we hate about the way we are, and what we should change in order to feel satisfied with ourselves. We know what procedures, habits, routines, or approaches would serve us best in pursuing our goals. Goals that, moreover, we're confident we're capable of achieving: losing weight, exercising, quitting smoking, being more affectionate with our partners, learning Spanish, being more attentive to our loved ones, spending more quality time with the people we care about instead of lounging around in bed or on the couch, trying to learn something new each dawning day. We all know these things would improve our lives in one way or another, and yet—without fully understanding why—we fail to do them.

We are paradoxical and occasionally contradictory creatures, and this fundamental characteristic of the human condition is one of the many reasons why a robot would have such a difficult time acting and behaving as we do.

Some people have learned to deal with their internal contradictions quite well by rationalizing them into a behavioral model that is coherent—in other words, not contradictory. People are said to be coherent when what they think, what they say, and what they do all converge within the same sphere. There is no contradiction or difficulty in understanding themselves. Or, at least, it doesn't seem that way. It's entirely likely that we have examples of these types of people all around us.

If we make proper use of the critical thinking switch, we can live within a certain degree of logic and avoid falling victim so often to these internal contradictions. Let's look at an example: Life as a couple, whether as newlyweds or while dating, is mostly a wonderful experience, a positive process of getting to know both the other person and yourself better. It's a time of fun, passion, discovery, and attentiveness toward each other. It's an attempt to please the other person, to make him or her feel happy and appreciated. You try to put your best self on full display, to put your best foot forward, to be the best version of yourself you can be, and to show the other person how far you're willing to go. In short, you focus your attention on the other person and hope for reciprocity. Suddenly, after a couple years of blissful cohabitation—where the only responsibility you had was working and paying rent, where there were no commitments to anyone or anything, where vacations, weekends, and even the occasional weeknight were spent doing whatever you wanted, like going out for dinner, catching a concert or a Broadway show, visiting a historic site—you one day wake up and think how great it would be to become parents, how wonderful it would be to bring a baby into this world and start a family. And, less than a year later, after a shared journey of excitement throughout the pregnancy, the baby is born and you become parents. Well, according to the statistics, this couple today has a 50 percent chance of divorcing before that baby turns five years old. It's highly possible that this marriage won't survive in the long term. Why? Have they stopped loving each other?

The answer is a complex one, but our contradictory nature can help us understand this question. If they didn't flip the critical thinking switch at the right time, and if they still haven't done so as parents, it's reasonable to expect that things won't go as planned. It's because many couples consider parenthood through the same lens as they did their dating or newlywed life: Through the happiness that comes from only needing to dedicate time and attention to your partner and to yourself, of having no other responsibility than doing what you want, when you want, with the person you love.

Without realizing it, we've come to view the future of parenting through the lens of an optimistic present. But a baby radically disrupts life's patterns, and our criteria for caring about our partner and ourselves are affected by a third, more demanding standard: the baby. Lacking sufficient reflection, we start to feel that life is slipping away from what it used to be, that the hedonism we enjoyed is beginning to fade, and oftentimes we're not ready for that. We want to be fantastic parents and have picture-perfect families, but we also harbor desires to enjoy life as we did before. We want to have a wonderful, stable partner who loves and remains faithful to us, but we also want to be open to other experiences outside of marriage. We want to spend time with our family, with our children, watching them grow. But we also want to develop ourselves individually, both professionally and recreationally.

There are so many demands, hopes, dreams, and aspirations, and we want to fulfill them all. We're not willing to sacrifice anything, which demonstrates that—even though we know it's impossible—we keep trying. Lipovetsky has written one of the best contemporary essays in terms of helping us understand the lifestyle we're leading and the kind of society we are building. It's titled "Paradoxical Happiness," and although it was published in 2006, many of the analyses it presents are completely relevant today.

Understanding ourselves—knowing who we are—while at the same time understanding those around us means accepting their contradictions and trying to cope with them as best we can, because we all carry within us wonderfully paradoxical imperfections.

We live in a society that, on the one hand, celebrates hedonism in nearly every aspect of life. Pleasure for pleasure's sake, sex without any burdensome moral codes, food everywhere, fun, alcohol, parties, constant travel, an obsession with new experiences . . . But, on the other hand, this hedonistic pursuit of worldly pleasures clashes with the most powerful preventive ideology of all: The one that tries to lead us away from our vices, that demonizes tobacco and promotes exercise as part of a healthy lifestyle, that gets annual medical checkups and blood tests just as a precaution, that monitors our diet in an almost mathematically obsessive way through calorie-counting apps, that signs up for meditation classes in search of emotional balance.

We're living in a time when the paradoxical extremes seem to coexist with complete normalcy. While we force ourselves to take care and be well, to make sacrifices in many personal aspects in pursuit of a healthier life, we're also constantly trying to hedonistically indulge in pleasures that aren't good for us, for our health. In case it's still not quite clear, we are often contradictory beings, and if we switch on our critical thinking skills, we're also able to understand other people's contradictions as well, which can help us live together in greater harmony.

ELEVEN

Victoria Camps: Post-Truth, and In Praise of Doubt

If we want to think properly—if we want to develop a sieve-like way of thinking, one that can separate the proverbial wheat from the chaff—then we cannot overlook one of the most important tools we have at our disposal: doubt. There should be a mandatory subject in schools and every other educational endeavor that teaches us the healthy exercising of doubt. Doubt is something that has to be learned. That last statement might sound silly, trivial, or even foolish. You might think that we don't need to be taught how to doubt because it's something we learn on our own, and yet nothing could be further from the truth. Learning to doubt, knowing when to doubt, knowing how to doubt, and living with certain doubts, and yet—despite it all—living happy and balanced lives is essential for our personal development.

We live surrounded—bombarded, if you ask me—by an overflow of information that we have to deal with each and every day. All of a sudden, we're hit with a countless number of headlines, notifications, events, opinions that seem like truths, truths that seem like opinions . . . and if that weren't enough, we now find ourselves living in the "post-truth era." As if the daily pressure of our own internal contradictions combined with those of other people wasn't already enough—you only live once, so live life to the fullest and enjoy each and every experience . . . but take care of yourself, be cautions, and think about the future—we now have to add this notion of "post-truth" to the mix. Post-truth became a buzzword in 2016, and I'm afraid it's going to stick with us for quite some time.

Post-truth explains the current circumstance in which objective facts have less influence on the formation of public opinion than appeals to emotions and personal beliefs. It is the most effective tool that liars have at their disposal. These are new techniques for deception that have been honed to perfection, especially through social media. It's an emotional lie designed to create and shape public opinion; it's a sensationalist form of manipulation in search of an emotional response while abandoning all semblance of objectivity. And, of course, it makes the possibility of ascertaining the facts of the matter exponentially more difficult.

While it's no recent phenomenon for someone in a position of power to want to control public opinion, what is new is how deeply these emotional lies have become rooted in the populous, especially in a generation that is supposedly the most highly educated in history. Paradoxically, we find that steering public opinion in an era rife with options for media outlets, where access to information is just a click away, is a piece of cake. What's concerning is that we can be so easily manipulated, that all it takes is a sensational headline or a few shocking or semi-scandalous images for us to internalize the opinion they want us to adopt. But what's even more alarming is that we don't even question the objectivity of facts, the objectivity of the news. On the contrary, we assume without the slightest hint of doubt that the things we're told are true and happen exactly as they are presented to us or, at the very least, we make no effort to verify them even though we have the means to do so. This is why it's essential that we teach our children, our young people, and even those of us who aren't so young anymore, the value of learning through doubt.

Post-truth—that is, a well-told lie that conveys a sense of truth while directly appealing to a human being's emotional side—is more advantageous than any other truth when it comes to shaping opinions. And for this post-truth, a series of mechanisms and instruments are being developed to facilitate its ability to spread everywhere. Post-truth is finding it extremely easy to establish itself among us, but what's worse is that it's become entrenched in the social and intellectual landscape, eliminating its worst enemy—critical thinking—in order to remain present among us for quite some time. It's one of the greatest threats we face as a society because it goes almost completely unnoticed. It feeds on the hyper-connectivity between individuals, a hyper-connectivity that's become something of a refuge for freedom, albeit one in which the power structures have managed to infiltrate without our realizing it. Almost imperceptibly, social media has become a post-truth lackey. News and headlines are produced, along with images, a bit of text rife with emotion, and shared who knows how many times. Armies of hackers, subsidized by political and/or economic interests, flood the internet with fake news each and every day. It's truly astonishing how news with the thinnest semblance of truth can be retweeted or posted on Facebook so simply and uncritically.

The instruments used by post-truth paradoxically become our allies when it's time to defend our freedoms, and post-truth takes advantage of this confusion to slip through the cracks of public opinion. In a society of turbo-temporality, people are increasingly interested in spreading a message as swiftly as possible rather than in pausing to reflect on its objectivity and veracity.

A society that doesn't actively engage in critical thinking, that doesn't question the things happening all around it, becomes a post-truth collaborationist society, a post-truth comrade, an ally in the defense of credible and sentimental lies. This is why we must reclaim doubt if we want to improve the society in which we live and recover something that seems to be increasingly out of favor: authenticity. Authenticity is losing the battle against the superficial, against the virtual.

In 2016, Victoria Camps, one of Spain's leading thinkers in the field of political philosophy and a specialist in ethics, published a book that highlights this need: *In Praise of Doubt.* She isn't the first philosopher, male or female, to champion the need for doubt in order to improve not only ourselves but also our world. From its very beginnings, the history of philosophy has upheld doubt as a necessary tool as well as—or perhaps even more so—as a lifestyle.

Why should doubt even exist in today's times? Camps suggest the following answer:

> "We live in a time of extremism, antagonism, and confrontation. On every level of every field, but especially in politics. An attitude that the media highlights at will and which escalates thanks to the ease with which social networks provide the opportunity to take a shot at anyone whose behavior or mere presence is uncomfortable . . . In a climate such as this, instead of an immediate outburst, expressing doubt in the face of what's disconcerting or strange would be a healthier way for everyone to react.

Take your time, think twice, and let a day or two go by before firing off an angry retort."

Adopting a perspective on life in which doubt plays a role, where doubt prevails over the empire of immediacy bearing down on us like a despot would be tremendously beneficial to our evolution as a species, to the building of a healthier society, at least in terms of its mental habits.

Doubt isn't fashionable, and it likely never will be as long as we remain immersed in the turbo-temporality that has engulfed our lives. Immediacy and instantaneousness have become mental habits that are expanding by leaps and bounds, aided and abetted by tools in the form of social networks that we've discussed. And, of course, in this context, doubt means slowing down, pausing to reflect, to investigate, to inquire, to take the time to see whether deception or manipulation is at play or if something is advantageous or harmful. From the perspective of today's society, doubt signifies deceleration. It requires time, which itself causes stress, because such time is seen as having been wasted.

It is becoming increasingly difficult to prioritize doubt over the visceral reaction demanded of us from every angle of society. And it's largely because having doubt implies taking a step back. This "stepping back" is a complicated task precisely because we're being sold a world of sensations and experiences above and beyond what comes with a rational, reflective society. Taking a step back means separating ourselves, not getting involved, not being part of something, all of which makes us uneasy because social media is constantly pushing us in the other direction, to participate and engage in everything, even if it's virtually, and doubt is far from an ideal companion in such situations.

Why don't we tend to doubt things? Professor Camps answers this question quite clearly: It's much easier to think dichotomously; that is, with two opposite poles. Yes and no, good and bad, beautiful and ugly. By rejecting any sense of nuance, this way of classifying reality is a great help in terms of simplifying things. When there are no shades of gray, we don't have to offer up any explanations about anything: it's either a simple yes or no:

> "It's easy to situate yourself as a 'Yes' or a 'No' because you don't need any argumentation in order to do so. I'm either pro-independence or pro-union. Right-wing or left-wing. I will or I will not accept refugees. Nuance requires too much effort. Doubt is an unsettling killjoy."

In other words, doubt is as uncomfortable as it is laborious. It involves a waste of both time and energy, and societal immediacy isn't inclined to promote such things. To this obstacle we can add another, perhaps more profound challenge in terms of analysis: to doubt is to admit that we don't know something, that we are imperfect, while the outward image we want to project is one of confidence, of having certainty on our side. Just go on any social media platform and see how the arguments presented always seem to be "definitive" ones. We demonstrate complete conviction in what we post there. Not only do we leave no room for doubt, we make a point of our absolute certainty. To do otherwise would be to show weakness, something that's not well received in today's society.

TWELVE

Pyrrho of Elis: Pragmatic Skepticism

Apart from Professor Camps's 2016 essay, we can find countless other examples of thinkers who have argued on behalf of the importance of doubt and advocated in favor of a particularly skeptical attitude as key to pursuing a worthy life's work. In the time of classical Greece, the importance of being skeptical rose to such levels that it even had its own school, headed by the man recognized as the father of skepticism: Pyrrho of Elis. To talk about Pyrrhonism is to present a model of thinking and living that can be useful to us in everyday matters.

Pyrrho, like Socrates, was *agraphos*—that is, he left no written works. What we do know about him comes from the testimony of third parties and direct disciples like Timon of Phlius and Sextus Empiricus, or from such illustrious ancient historians as Cicero and Diogenes Laërtius. The compilation of these testimonies has required, not only for Pyrrho of Elis but many other Greek philosophers, serious research into the sources to extract the most reliable interpretations possible.

There are few scholars more prominent in this field than Professor Ramón Román Alcalá, who specialized in ancient

Greek skepticism and, specifically, in the figure of Pyrrho of Elis. He is the author of the book *Pyrrho of Elis: A Penguin and a Rhinoceros in Wonderland.*

If Pyrrho is the father of skepticism, and skepticism is a posture based on doubt, then we can understand why Pyrrho left nothing in writing behind. For Professor Román, this is an entirely plausible hypothesis. Pyrrho, in being consistent with his philosophy of life, would not have wanted to dogmatize or indoctrinate anyone. But there is another possibility I would like to postulate, particularly when it comes to flipping the critical thinking switch. This notion is that perhaps Pyrrho left nothing in writing because he was convinced of the superiority of actions over words, of the supremacy that practical aspects of life hold over the theoretical.

This second interpretation seems perhaps closer to understanding why he left no written records behind. What matters is what you do, not what you think or say: It's actions over words. True skepticism lies in how someone lives life, not in the doctrines that speak to skepticism as a philosophy. During his lifetime, Pyrrho, along with his teacher Anaxarchus, accompanied Alexander the Great's expedition to Asia. It's not surprising that, having seen other worlds, encountered other cultures, and studied ways of life that were radically different from the Greek with heavy Eastern influences, on a journey where he met Persian priests, gymnosophists (naked sages), and even Brahmins, he came to realize the relativity and diversity of the world and ended up with a life of skepticism.

That's why this book you're reading—if you're to adopt the Pyrrhonian perspective on life—must, to be helpful, be reflected in your actions, in the reality of a way of thinking and acting that truly changes you. It's not an intellectual exercise in how to think about things, but rather *for* things, for use *in* things (understanding "things" as life itself).

In fact, Pyrrho was widely recognized as a great thinker in his day, most likely because of the lifestyle he led, which resulted in many others following him . . . hence the talk of a school of skepticism (though surely without the slightest pretense on Pyrrho's part). From what we know, Pyrrho was a great example for the society of the time because he possessed two qualities that stood out above the rest: intelligence and nobility. Moreover, to his contemporaries, both Pyrrho and those who later embraced skepticism were considered prudent and magnanimous individuals.

IMPRUDENCE AND PAMPLINAS

Proper thinking requires proper doubt, yes, but above all it requires knowing how to develop a skeptical attitude when the situation calls for it. This latter skill must be mastered if we are to achieve Pyrrhonian wisdom. One of the best lessons the skeptics teach us about our lives comes from the prudent attitude exemplified by Pyrrho.

Prudence comes from the Latin *prudentia*, which in turn is derived from *providentia*, meaning "one who sees ahead." Prudence is essential when facing certain situations in life, as it implies temperance, caution, moderation—in short, good judgment. But prudence is, primarily, a reflective attitude when confronting a problematic situation because to be prudent means engaging your analytical abilities and knowing how to distinguish the good from the bad, the beneficial from the harmful. If we extend this application to the twenty-first century, it certainly wouldn't be a bad idea to adopt a prudent attitude toward the lifestyles being hyperbolically advertised to us with every passing minute of the day.

Adopting a prudent attitude in the Pyrrhonian style would be no small achievement. To this step, we can add a second vital quality for leading a good life, one that became a paradigm for skeptics: imperturbability of character, which we will explore in greater detail in a later section (see chapter 27). But what does this mean? Something as simple as not letting every trivial or insignificant thing upset you or otherwise alter your character. When faced with the multiplicity of theories, presumptions, prejudices, and virtualized models of wonderful lives that end up causing us nothing but frustration, the best thing is to don a sort of armor so that nothing can affect us. Don't let speculation, fantasies, and unfounded theories about life, happiness, success, motivation, or creativity generate any anxiety that would keep us up at night. We must maintain a calmness of spirit, aware that there is no single solution to all life's ills, no philosopher's stone for happiness. With skeptics, what matters most is that this attitude becomes an existing practice in your life.

The question, then, is how such a feat might be achieved. The best way is to train one's character in the use of a very significant tool for the skeptics: ataraxia, which is nothing more than profound peace of mind. In this sense, doubt is essential to understanding the skeptics' process, as Professor Román rightly points out:

> "Pyrrhonian doubt also intervenes in the realm of opinions, which is why Pyrrho renounces them in favor of his aspirations to ataraxia: if we can aspire to peace of mind, we cannot allow ourselves to be caught up in the whirlwind of philosophical debates."

The question is simple: How do we manage to remain calm if we live in this world of hyperstimulation, where we're being constantly bombarded with millions of offers, both material and emotional, and where information overload has reached such a degree that we're left with an ever more unsettled mind? One of the most useful pieces of advice these skeptics offer us is to avoid entering into speculative discussions, to steer clear of unfounded opinions being bandied about, and to avoid other worthless pitfalls in order to better cultivate a calm and peaceful spirit. As we mentioned before, all you have to do is look around and you'll see that emotional imbalances are increasing exponentially—imbalances that indicate we're failing to achieve the coveted peace of mind, that we're unable to distinguish what's truly important from what isn't.

Like Pyrrho, we must learn to not get bogged down in concerns, arguments, or battles over the countless trivialities on which we waste our time and energy. We turn what is primarily anecdotal into something problematic, drowning ourselves in unnecessary anxiety when we could actually be living a much more tranquil life. If we think about it carefully, we'll end up realizing that we devote so much time and effort—untold hours of consternation and even anguish—to things that don't deserve it, to things that, where I'm from, we call *pamplinas*: nonsense.

It's important to emphasize that Pyrrho's skepticism is an attitude he arrived at, not so much a starting point. In other words, through life experiences, with the critical thinking switch always engaged, he gradually realized how difficult it is to truly, profoundly know things, as well as the impossibility of this endeavor. He concluded that racking his brain over unsolvable issues and debating opinions caused him more harm than good, and as such he adopted the skeptical attitude. We mustn't forget that Pyrrho wanted to be happy, and to achieve this, he uncovered something we could well apply to ourselves here in the twenty-first century: To be happy, we must live calmly and serenely, at peace with our fellow human beings, but most of all, with ourselves. And the best way to do this is to practice it daily, to accept that life unfolds as it does, it is what it is, and that there are some things we must do while others can be discarded.

To this Pyrrhonian sense of skepticism, it wouldn't be a bad idea to add one last, extremely useful element when it comes to our quest for that peace of mind for which we so desperately long in this constantly unsettling world: aphasia.

Aphasia is nothing more than the "suspension of judgment." No judgments being made, no opinions being given. This is an essential tool for achieving the tranquility—ataraxia—that we yearn for. In a society such as ours, where we live life on the edge of our seats, like shots ready to be fired at social media posts. We find ourselves outraged by other people's opinions and react by lobbing volleys of our own, constantly in search of arguments to support them, waging a war to win the debate. And it's not the first time that the consequences of charging forward with our opinions end up with feelings of discomfort and anxiety because they weren't well received or otherwise didn't hit the intended target. In this regard, Pyrrho was clear: If you want to achieve that ideal of a peaceful life with yourself and others—serene of spirit, calm of intellect—then avoid exchanges of opinions and, if you can, try not to issue judgments that might end up coming back to harm you.

THIRTEEN

Montaigne: Self-Esteem, or Thinking Highly of Oneself

The school of skepticism that emerged after Pyrrho of Elis's departure left a legacy of renowned followers and notable admirers interspersed throughout history, and there's much we can learn from all of them, especially when it comes to achieving the goal of leading a good life. One of the most unique among them is someone we've already discussed: the French thinker and father of the essay as a genre, Michel de Montaigne. Montaigne is the first thinker who transformed everything he analyzed into philosophy; he believed deeply in philosophy as a way of life, and that the events surrounding it can and should be examined through the lens of this discipline. Nothing should be able to escape the microscope of what we've been referring to as "the flipping of the critical thinking switch."

Instead of bringing life closer to a philosophical analysis and writing a treatise on existential questions, Montaigne went for the opposite approach: bringing philosophy closer not only to life in general, but to the common, everyday life that anyone among us might lead. He paid attention to each and every quotidian detail, and it's no coincidence that he confesses in his *Essays* that the primary object of examination will be himself.

He is known as history's first "essayist." Before Montaigne, most writings related to philosophy or theology tended to be quite systematic, organized along thematic lines depending on the subject or object being investigated. Fields of knowledge were delimited, and one could say there was a specialization for each of them. But all of a sudden, at the age of thirty-eight, after having twice served as mayor of Bordeaux, Montaigne decided to retire to his château and write. A problem arose while searching for topics to write about, at which point he decided to try something revolutionary for the historical moment in which he lived. He decided to write about what he knew best: himself. He makes this clear in the preface to his *Essays*:

> "Thus, reader, myself am the matter of my book: there's no reason thou shouldst employ thy leisure about so frivolous and vain a subject."

He decided to write about himself, about what he'd learned during his life, about what he'd experienced, about the themes that interested him, yet without being obliged to research or thoroughly address what other thinkers had previously said on these topics, though he did so without rejecting the opportunity to enter into dialogue with them, whether they were Greek or Roman philosophers, poets, historians, and so forth.

What's particularly interesting about Montaigne's *Essays* is that, unlike the prevailing philosophical model of the time, this book explores the human condition in the most natural way possible, addressing issues that any ordinary person might have. His *Essays* were, and still are, widely admired, read, and studied.

He didn't want to leave out any aspect of our world, and so, interestingly enough, he came to write about the penis and its importance with regard to the notion of virility. On this topic, he wrote the following:

> "Every one of my parts, each as much as another, makes me myself. I owe to the public my complete portrait."

To achieve this, he uses every instrument at his disposal: reason and experience, without favoring one over the other.

> "There is no Desire more natural than that of Knowledge: We try all Ways that can lead us to it; where Reason is wanting, we therein employ Experience which is a Means much more weak and cheap. But Truth is so great a thing, that we ought not to disdain any Mediation that will guide us to it."

In other words, all the tools we have are valid for life. We don't have to discard any of them. But what's remarkable about Montaigne—what made him famous—is that, by using himself as the object of investigation and in deciding to do so in the form of a loosely structured book with scarcely any classification, he created an entirely new literary genre that he called, in French, the *essai*: A word that already implies a degree of skepticism in the approach to knowledge. It is a test, an attempt that helps us to understand ourselves better. Montaigne concerned himself with the analysis of personal experience; he believed that one learns more from oneself than from others, and so he tells us:

> "I had rather understand myself well in myself, than in Cicero. Of the experience I have of myself, I find enough to make me wise, if I were but a good scholar."

If we want to live a good life, the underlying goal is to learn how to think well. And for Montaigne to achieve this, everyday life became the focus of his research. He believed it was both necessary and interesting to investigate common matters; thus, as Victoria Camps explains, what mattered to Montaigne was a simple life filled with anecdotes. He studied the classics, yes, but when it came to the primary object of his observation, he focused on himself. He believed that anything could be a source of knowledge—the way he slept, how he protected himself from the cold, his bowel movements, his moments of pleasure. He dismissed no topic as it related to life, and what's of the greatest relevance to us is that he dismissed nothing that had to do with the self.

One of the problems we can analyze effectively using Montaigne's teachings is self-esteem; that is, the way we value or critique ourselves, which is generally rather harsh. Because of this persistent harshness we impose on ourselves, we often end up feeling distress and disappointment. When it comes to analyzing this problem, Montaigne can be of particular help. According to this particular intellectual, we have three major concerns from which we find it difficult to free ourselves.

First, we tend to be overly concerned about how we perceive our own bodies. We never fully accept ourselves. It's surprising that, when we read interviews with people we consider the epitome of beautiful—runway or magazine models, for example—many of them will share aspects of their physique they don't particularly like. We're far too critical of our bodies, and this disappointment—this inability for us to accept ourselves—can, depending on its intensity, cause serious problems that go beyond simple complexes and insecurities.

To address this, there are partial solutions to reshaping certain parts of our bodies that are within our reach. But if it were that simple, we would all have an enviable physique, and yet we don't. Some of us aren't happy with our hair or our nose, we don't really like our ears, our mouth is too wide or too thin, our lips aren't full enough, our eyelashes are too short, or our eyebrows are either too high, too low, or droop over our eyelids. The point is that, while we can try to partially modify our body with diet, exercise, or surgery, there are other factors we cannot control and for which we are not responsible. Height, skin color, the distance between our eyes—there is almost nothing we can do about these such imponderable features.

The second point Montaigne raises as a personal concern is our limited ability to accept being judged by others in ways with which we don't agree. The negative, destructive judgment is the one we fail to assimilate. It's the uncomfortable feeling when others don't accept us as we are, when they don't approve of how we're tackling life, when they disagree with our habits or customs, with our personal relationships, with our choice of friends, partners, jobs . . . Often, if we're not getting social reinforcement in these areas, feelings of discomfort start welling up inside us.

The final feeling about ourselves that Montaigne identifies as important for building a healthy, and, if possible, less self-conscious personality is that of intelligence. We tend to judge ourselves in comparison to others based on how smart we seem. We always want to have a greater capacity for intellect than we do, and as a result, we suffer, aware of the fact that we can't expand beyond our limitations.

These are three of the factors that make us feel uncomfortable with ourselves. This way of tearing down our self-esteem stems from choosing the wrong role models to look up to, thanks to a failure to consider either their nature or our own. This is why, to develop the balanced personality we all want to achieve—a personality that knows where the critical thinking switch is located and when to turn it on—we must choose carefully whom we admire. If we don't, it's highly likely that we'll fall into a state of deep sadness or even depression every time we fail to measure up to the role models we've chosen for our life. Making the wrong decision without taking into account our own circumstance, attitudes, and abilities can ruin us.

One way to avoid choosing the wrong model and trying not to disappoint ourselves is to pay attention to the simple details of the people around us, the people who go about their lives doing ordinary things without needing much of anything else to feel happy: a beer with friends at the neighborhood bar, a quiet bit of evening reading in the armchair, a short nap on the sofa before starting the afternoon's activities, a morning walk to school with the children, chatting about everyday things.

Montaigne's *Essays* were so successful because, among other things, they spoke about the everyday life of each person. About the search for simplicity. Problems arise when we're made to believe that we are unique, one of a kind, and, above all, extraordinary. The progression from individualism to the extremes of hyper-individualism stirs in us the unconscious need to feel like unique beings, like we're not just becoming part of the pack. The message being sent by this hypermodern society always revolves around the exceptional: the finest people, stunning images, distinctive beauties, unique restaurants, breathtaking landscapes, thrilling experiences . . . and then, of course, we all of a sudden look into the mirror and do a bit of self-analysis only to realize that we're nothing out of the ordinary, complete with all the consequences for self-esteem that this realization brings.

Our obsession with the singular, with the exclusive, ends up taking a heavy toll on us . . . so heavy, in fact, that we eventually come to despise what's truly important and vital within us: the ordinary, the repetitive. As Ortega y Gasset said, man is a creature of habit. Normality has become a serious psychological burden that leaves us feeling unhappy, even miserable, simply because we're not living the life we've been sold: the extraordinary life.

The mistake we're actually making is rejecting the routine. "Routine" has taken on a stigma, it's become synonymous with boring, dull, insipid. For many people, it represents passivity, stagnation, and the mundane. But if we flip on the critical thinking switch, we'll realize that, to be happy, we must become the architects of our own routines. Few things bring greater satisfaction, calmness, and serenity than a routine we've designed for ourselves.

If we want to regain happiness and increase self-esteem, we're obliged to value the routine, the ordinary, to build a day-to-day life where we can find moments and spaces in which we can feel simply happy. Otherwise, if we're constantly waiting for something extraordinary to arrive, waves of suffering will likely be on the horizon.

As Michel de Montaigne said, "The greatest misfortune for us is to disdain what we are." Part of who we are is defined by what we do, which is why it's not advisable to show disdain for our everyday lives. By discussing ordinary and even trivial topics like flatulence or impotence, Montaigne elevates the intellectual value of life's vulgarity, making it both relatable and worthy of analysis.

FOURTEEN

Solid Thinking: The Importance of Context

We must take control of our lives, and while this may seem obvious, nothing could be further from the truth. We're living in reverse: Life is what steers us, not the other way around. In this tyranny of hyperactivity, we let ourselves be carried along instead of following with intent.

To explain the importance of control in our lives, it's necessary to understand the circumstance and to attempt to choose the contexts. To help clarify this, we'll look at an experiment conducted at Oxford University with a group of ten-month-old babies. They were placed in a room together, and every so often an external red light would turn on. At first, the babies, astonished by the light outside their room, would smile in amazement at this phenomenon. But after it had happened a few times, they stopped paying attention. A second group of babies was then introduced into the same room, but with the added variable that the red light only turned on when the babies made a certain movement. When the babies figured out how it worked, things got pretty wild in that room as they kept turning the red light on again and again, extending the playful game almost three times longer than the first test group. When the babies discovered what needed to be done to turn on the light and were successful in doing so, they experienced the satisfaction of being able to control their context. Controlling or even just knowing how the elements around you operate, coupled with understanding the people around you, is the first step to understanding the context in which you operate.

Context is essential, and we must learn to recognize it from a young age if we are going to look beyond what we do and broaden our horizons beyond what's immediately in front of us. Every circumstance we analyze will help us approach it in a more balanced way.

In philosophy classes, we always begin by studying the authors' contexts—the historical, cultural, and philosophical contexts—because to understand how people think, how they face and interpret the world, and to better understand their philosophy, it's necessary to understand their contexts and circumstance. When reading philosophy with students, whether it's Plato, Aristotle, or Nietzsche himself, we can't start directly with the works even though that's something that can be done at any point. If we want to better understand why they write what they write—why, for example, Nietzsche's philosophy is so compelling, so powerful in its sentence structure and phrasing, why he truly revolutionized the art of thinking—we'll have a much easier time if we know a little more about how he grew up, if we know that his father was a priest who died bedridden after a year of tremendous pain and suffering when Nietzsche was only five years old. He was a child who saw his father, who was a good person and servant of God, suffer such unbearable physical torment for so long, an experience so very difficult to comprehend for someone who loses a paternal figure under such circumstance.

Nietzsche retired early, before his fortieth birthday, because he suffered from severe migraines and rheumatism. During the final ten years of his life, he had to be admitted to a psychiatric facility because he had trouble controlling himself. Trying to understand Nietzsche within his context is not the same as doing so without it, and knowing this affords us a different perspective on the writer's philosophy.

This is not to say that context or circumstance justify everything. We can't rely on context when something doesn't go well, when we haven't made the right decision. Context helps us better understand and situate ourselves in life, but we still have to be ready to flip the critical thinking switch when it comes time to make decisions.

Introducing context into the practice of critical thinking is essential. Contextualization is one of the best philosophical habits we should be introducing into our lives, a habit that ought to be systematized almost mechanically, placing everything in context, in its time, in its moment. Having the ability to see past the tip of our own nose, beyond the limits of our own sensitivities, and to try to grasp and understand what's around us.

These are difficult times for understanding context because we are awash in what Lipovetsky calls "the age of hyper-individualism," during which the individual takes precedence over everything else. Concern for oneself has become the central axis of our lives; thus, in a society driven by the constant pursuit of personal pleasure, the tyranny of happiness prevails. This hyper-individuality doesn't usually initiate the perspective of context, so when we're making decisions, we're often not able to adequately consider our surroundings. These are not good times for "the Other," because we're not taking context into account. If we want to lead a more balanced life, we must engage the critical thinking switch without forgetting this particular element.

Context helps us to better understand both ourselves and others. If we want the decisions we make to be as accurate as possible, we need to analyze contexts, particularly our own. As the saying goes, it's unwise to make decisions "in the heat of the moment" when emotions are running high and rational thought is barely even present. We feel the urge to make a decision right then and there, convincing ourselves that this is the best course of action, but we know that later, in a calmer state of mind, we'll analyze the situation and see everything more clearly, having taken into account the context and circumstance that we may have overlooked or the details we'd forgotten during that impulsive moment.

Today's prevailing lifestyle is instantaneous, fast, and fleeting, one in which patience, reflection, and analysis are no longer the norm. This turbo-temporality is another great enemy of context. The need to do everything quickly, to have everything instantly, to achieve things almost immediately prevents us from analyzing the circumstance surrounding each and every moment. This is why we must learn to think both critically and calmly, to recognize that there's more than just "me," "myself," and "I." And, to do this, we will turn to one of the most important Spanish philosophers of all time: Ortega y Gasset.

FIFTEEN

Ortega y Gasset: Circumstance for the Twenty-First Century

Ortega y Gasset (1883–1955) has secured his place in textbooks on the history of philosophy. He stands out as one of the most lucid, clear-sighted, and accessible thinkers ever when it comes to engaging with his texts, which may well be due to the fact that he began his career as a journalist. He's one of those writers who doesn't get lost in the dense, technical, almost scientific vocabulary that characterizes so many philosophers and often alienates the general public. Ortega y Gasset is a pleasure to read because his expositions are tremendously clear. I suppose this garnered him a certain amount of suspicion when it comes to the pantheon of "Pure Philosophers," the result of which is that he is often placed among the ranks of essayists. When it comes to Spain, it could be argued that he never quite received the recognition that a thinker of his caliber deserves. As the saying goes, no one is a prophet in their own land.

Ortega y Gasset was born in Madrid in 1883. His father was primarily a journalist, though he authored a number of socially themed novels that were published without much fanfare. As a journalist, he worked for the newspaper *El Imparcial*, which was owned by Ortega y Gasset's mother, Dolores Gasset. His was a classical liberal family of late-nineteenth-century Spain. Writing ran in the blood of both his father's and mother's sides of the family. As a young man, he witnessed what became known as the Disaster of '98, in which Spain lost the colonies of Cuba, the Philippines, and Puerto Rico. In 1905, he graduated with a degree in philosophy from the Universidad Complutense de Madrid. Two years later, he earned his doctorate, and set off to visit German universities in search of what he called the regeneration of Spain. The fact that he spent part of his life abroad, specifically Germany, was crucial in terms of shaping the pro-European vision of Spain he championed throughout his life.

At twenty-eight, Ortega y Gasset married Rosa Spottorno, and in 1911, he began to develop a personal interest in participating in the public life of his country, in particular a turbulent Madrid, where winds of change were in the air. In 1914, he published his first book, *Meditations on Quixote*, in which he expressed his ideas about the importance of perspective when it comes to approaching life. He was the founding editor of a number of magazines, perhaps the most renowned of which was the *Revista de Occidente*, which became a social and cultural instrument aimed at the dictatorship of Miguel Primo de Rivera (1923), a stance that led him to resign his professorship from the Universidad Complutense de Madrid in 1929. In 1931, with the proclamation of the Second Republic, he was elected deputy to the Constituent Assembly. However, following the 1936 coup d'état that led to the Spanish Civil War, he went into exile: a journey that led him through Argentina, Paris, the Netherlands, and Portugal. In 1945, after the end of World War II, he returned to Spain, but was unable to regain his professorship. A few years later, he decided to move to Germany, where he was warmly welcomed and received well-deserved recognition within the academic world. In 1955, he finally returned once again to Spain, where he died later that same year.

This brief contextual biography serves as an introduction to a man quite unlike the image we usually picture in our mind when thinking of a philosopher. A person dedicated to the society of his time and determined to fight to improve the world in which they lived. A fighter who attacked from all angles: on the intellectual level through the publication of books and essays as well as founding educational centers and journals, and on the social level, through his contributions to his country's journalistic and political life. In short, a committed individual who was forced into exile on a number of occasions throughout his life because he didn't fit into the prevailing political and social models and who garnered recognition abroad, including honorary doctorates awarded to him by the Universities of Glasgow and Marburg. His life, the varied countries in which he lived, the cultures in which he immersed himself during his journeys, all this helps us better understand his philosophical outlook. It's no wonder that his most famous quote—"I am myself and my circumstance"—can be more fully understood when we're aware of some of the circumstances surrounding the life of this remarkable Spanish thinker.

That phrase, which encapsulates part of his thinking, first appears in his book, *Meditations on Quixote.* Logically, we cannot distill this extraordinary figure's entire philosophy to a single sentence, but we can gain a better understanding of his work by delving a bit deeper into what this meant and the advantages we can draw from this thought process for our own day-to-day lives.

For Ortega y Gasset, we are not who we are if we don't take our circumstances into account. The self cannot be understood in isolation; our identity is not constructed independent of the things, people, places, events, and so on, that surround us.

Circumstances can be understood as the sum of all these things that help us to become ourselves. When Ortega y Gasset says, "If I do not save that, I do not save myself," he is expressing the need to consider the circumstances of our lives in order to better understand ourselves. Hence, the importance of always situating ourselves within the context of our circumstances. Problems arise when we forget our own circumstances or imagine ourselves surrounded by others, because in such cases, we're simply falsifying our self.

When we're not engaging the critical thinking switch regarding our circumstances—when we're not reflecting on where we are, where we come from, where we're rooted, what our cultural or economic status is, and so on—we may well end up unwittingly fabricating them. It's like the low-income family, struggling financially, who takes on additional debt to buy a motorbike for a child who won't stop asking for one, or the latest-generation smartphone just like the ones wealthier people can afford, or to gift that child a trip to EuroDisney for the child's first communion, a trip that will take the family nearly two years to pay off by sacrificing other things that might have been more pressing, more necessary. These people are constructing a falsified self, one that cuts against their own present circumstances, and their identity will suffer serious challenges to self-acceptance because they've failed to do what Ortega y Gasset advises: saving the self while also saving the circumstances.

If you'll indulge me, we could touch a bit on the art of pretending, of faking, of what's commonly called "posturing" or being a "poseur." In this case, the circumstances are the reality that surrounds the subject. It's the requisite world in which the subject develops, the environment in which life unfolds, so that the circumstances aren't so much about all this is me but rather what shapes me, what comprises me, whether that is my place of birth, family, language, social class, beliefs, and so on. The self is inseparable from the circumstances, which is why it's so important to do something we often hear about from people who have found happiness: "Don't forget where you came from." Knowing your roots, your origins, is fundamental to shaping a stable, secure, deep-seated self. A "solid self," as I like to call it. The world in which I live cannot be different or distinct from me; it cannot be a reality independent of me, because if we want to better understand our world, we have to see it through the lens of our most authentic circumstances.

THE SELF AND THE AVATAR

What is happening to our circumstances here in the twenty-first century, when technology seems to occupy an ever-increasing part of our daily lives? Well, among other things, we're beginning to lend more importance to the virtual world than the real one. The time we spend interacting with the internet is growing exponentially, and the smartphone has become our most inseparable companion. We're starting to see and understand life—at least in part—through screens. The time spent socializing through screens is increasing to the point where, in many cases, it has surpassed real-life interactions. This fact is incredibly significant when it comes to understanding the direction in which our world is heading.

The circumstances surrounding our lives have changed radically over the last twenty years with the sudden arrival of not only globalization but, above all, the popularization of the internet. Without even realizing it, we've begun to feel, think about, and see the world from the perspective of these virtual circumstances, which have managed to rise to the same levels of intensity and depth as any real circumstances, and that's not even taking into account the growing phenomena of augmented reality glasses or virtual reality headsets.

This virtual circumstance is gaining ground, but what's worse is that it's starting to condition our real lives. If we were to update Ortega y Gasset's famous phrase, we would need to pluralize the word "circumstance" and thus it would become "I am myself and my circumstances" because, for some time now, we've had to reckon with two completely different circumstances: the real and the virtual. Personal and social relationships have two different sets of circumstances: On the one hand, we have models of personal relationships formed by our physical circumstances, but at the same time, we have virtual circumstances that offer us another form of social relationship, one not shaped by the physical but rather the virtual.

Life inevitably becomes more complicated because now we have to navigate two different sets of circumstances: One is real, where many of the circumstances are predefined, like where you were born, the neighborhood in which you grew up, the kind of parents you had, the teachers who passed through your life. The other one, the virtual circumstance, is characterized by having been chosen by you. You are the one who decides to join social networks, to consume the virtual reality of the online world, who chooses the apps and websites you want to use, whether to have Facebook, Instagram, LinkedIn, Twitter (now officially known as X), Tinder, or WhatsApp accounts, and to choose the people you accept within these virtual social networks.

All of which is to say that the virtual circumstance is chosen primarily by you, although the social pressure to be a part of it is quite strong itself. There are external circumstances constantly pushing us to participate in this world of virtual circumstances. And, of course, once you're inside, if you don't keep your critical thinking switch firmly in the "on" position, the consequences for the formation of the self can be devastating. To put it another way, the self in Ortega y Gasset's famous phrase would start to become less real—less shaped by its actual circumstances—and instead become a more virtual self.

The problem of achieving a solid, well-balanced personality, combined with the development of consistent thinking, arises when we begin to consider the possibility that the avatar we've created for the virtual personality we're constructing on social media—has started to take over the real emotions of the actual self: the one that has to wake up every morning and go to bed each night while in between interacting with itself and with other real individuals. We're enabling the virtual world to increasingly affect the real one.

Today, in the twenty-first century, we are seeing just how difficult it is to construct this self-identity: a difficulty unlike any we've seen before, due in part to the fact that our circumstances have doubled. The forging of self-identity is experiencing the most challenging historical moment it has ever faced because, on the one hand, it wants to experience a real, flesh-and-blood life, one that's satisfying and fully realized. But on the other hand, without even realizing it, virtual circumstances are causing this process of seeking out reality to be oriented more along virtual lines, and we're suffering greatly as a result. If you ask me, it's a voluntary suffering that begins the moment we allow ourselves to be significantly affected by virtual circumstances rather than actual ones. We're also similarly affected by others: As if dealing with our own two sets of circumstances on a daily basis—the real and the virtual—wasn't enough, we're also having to learn to live with those of others.

By doubling our personal circumstances (real and virtual), we're increasing the scope of action and attention, both on a personal level (dealing with both our real and virtual selves) and on a social level (dealing with other people's real and virtual personalities).

When we create our virtual circumstances, we accept the virtual circumstances of others, and that requires more of our time. When we activate the virtual self, we sometimes forget to do so from within our virtual circumstances. It's very important to follow a clear line of thought that associates:

Real Self—Real Circumstances
Virtual Self—Virtual Circumstances

Problems arise when these elements intersect and the real self is viewed from within virtual circumstances, or vice versa. If we focus on the virtual circumstances of others using our real self, we will be distorting our perspective and falsifying the circumstances, which will ultimately take a toll on us. And that's why, every time we turn on a screen and activate our virtual selves, we must remember to do so only from within our virtual circumstances.

THINKING WITH PERSPECTIVE

If we want to avoid so much suffering or becoming so angry, it's essential that we also bear in mind that others have their own set of circumstances, and that their "selves" are conditioned by those circumstances and we must learn to understand them. To better understand this topic, Ortega y Gasset produced the "Doctrine of the Point of View." He developed it as a theory on understanding the world, but we're going to apply it instead to our daily lives. This doctrine has also been called "perspectivism," and can best be summarized by the philosopher in his own words:

> "Two men may look, from different view-points, at the same landscape. Yet they do not see the same thing. Their different situations make the landscape assume two distinct types of organic structure in their eyes. The part which, in the one case, occupies the foreground, and is thrown into high relief in all its details, is, in the other case, the background, and remains obscure and vague in its appearance. Further, inasmuch as things which are put one behind the other are either wholly or partially concealed, each of the two spectators will perceive portions of the landscape which elude the attention of the other. Would there be any sense in either declaring the other's view of the landscape false? Evidently not; the one is as real as the other. But it would be just as senseless if, when our spectators found that their views of the landscape did not agree, they concluded that both views were illusory. Such a conclusion would involve belief in the existence of a third landscape, an authentic one, not subject to the same conditions as the other two. Well, an archetypal landscape of this kind does not and cannot exist. Cosmic reality is such that it can only be seen in a single definitive perspective. Perspective is one of the component parts of reality."

For Ortega y Gasset, the sum of perspectives was better than having only your own, which is why it's important to learn to enrich ourselves with others' perspectives. In fact, he applied this to his own life when he declared:

> "I have to be, at the same time, a university professor, a man of letters, a journalist, a politician, a café conversationalist, a bullfighter, a man of the world, something like a parish priest, and I don't know how many other things."

The problem is that, owing to the direction this society is taking, we are becoming increasingly obsessed with paying attention only to our inner voice, to our self, to ourselves. The hyper-individualists aren't willing to listen to others. All we want is to be heard, to impose our own perspective, but we aren't willing to pay attention to others.

Reality, obviously, presents us with multiple perspectives, and these are determined by each individual's circumstances. If we can understand this, we can be more understanding of others, of the things happening around us. Similarly, we can come to know that reality is enriched by the multitude of points of view we have on it. This is why it's advisable to not always be anchored to the same perspective. It's a good idea to change the TV channel or radio station in order to gain some diversity. It's a good idea to listen to and analyze different political parties in order to get a feel for the multiplicity of their positions and proposals. It's a good idea to reach out to others who don't necessarily think as we do and learn about their circumstances. If we follow Ortega y Gasset's advice, we'll be moving closer to reality, enriching our world, and broadening the actionable range of our critical thinking skills.

For Ortega y Gasset, the sum of the points of view—of the perspectives—provided us with a more authentic glimpse of reality. Given this, we might think that the doubling of the circumstances—the real and the virtual—could easily be a positive element in the pursuit of that authenticity. And he wouldn't be wrong, if we can give each of them their due value.

The problem arises when we fail to focus on what we should, and as such, our perception of life is out of focus. There's a Woody Allen film, *Deconstructing Harry*, in which one of the protagonists loses focus, and yet he doesn't realize it until those around him point it out. The issue in our virtual world is that no one tells you that you're unfocused, and the blurriness that begins in the virtual world eventually takes a toll in real life.

We're seeing the world out of focus. This is one of the most pressing problems of our current era. Not long ago, we focused on things close at hand, things we saw clearly. We were clear about where we wanted to go, about where we were headed. We focused our energies and efforts on clear, simple, transparent goals. Life—as well as the plan for living it—always ended up coming into focus sooner or later. The worst that could happen was that we'd have to change our focus, we'd have to set our sights on something different because life's circumstances had predisposed us in such a way. But, even during moments of crisis, we could always refocus somewhere else clearly and transparently.

Nowadays, this process has become much more difficult. Suddenly we no longer know where to focus in order to guide our lives, and so we're constantly looking every which way in search of reference points. Each of these reference points we focus on is scattered and diffuse, and when we do focus, we still can't see clearly what we want. We can't recognize the contours, the limits of the space in which we're moving, hence the disorientation we see every day in people who don't know how to orient their lives.

The thing is, the compass isn't broken. The guiding compass still works perfectly well. It still points north; it hasn't wavered. The challenge is that we don't know if we want to go north, not only because we can't focus with the necessary clarity, but also because we're terrified of what we'll find there. We can't properly focus our lives in any particular direction, whether it be a healthy personal relationship, a wholesome parenting model, a satisfying work relationship, a peaceful retirement. We just aren't seeing it clearly.

SIXTEEN

Aristotle: How to Control Anxiety

We are living in a strangely paradoxical time. It is, perhaps, the most complicated time in history in which to be happy, but we also have more tools than ever to facilitate access to that happiness. With all our vital needs met, we can allow ourselves to think about the future, yet when we do, problems arise. We have increasing knowledge about how human emotions work, but we're struggling more than ever to rid ourselves of the most harmful ones. Yes, we're surrounded by countless instruments, tools, and devices that make our lives more comfortable, and still we're almost constantly feeling uncomfortable with ourselves and with the world around us. What, exactly, is going on that's preventing us from being completely satisfied when the necessary instruments for satisfaction are all within our reach? Well, we'd need an encyclopedia-sized book to fully analyze that, so here we'll attempt to highlight a few of the more pressing problems, consider the responses many of history's greatest thinkers have offered, and see if there's something we can change about the way we're approaching life.

There's a very interesting study, conducted by Carl Benedikt Frey and Michael Osborne of Oxford University, that aims to anticipate how different jobs will evolve over the coming years. The idea is to predict, using the data we have on technological progress, how many of today's jobs could be automated (i.e., subject to automation) and thus be mechanized. After analyzing more than seven hundred jobs, they concluded that nearly 50 percent of them could potentially be performed by robots. So, if we want to prepare ourselves for the future, we need to be thinking about what jobs in which workers cannot be replaced by machines, and here we find a field in which it not only seems unlikely that workers could be replaced by robots but also is increasingly in demand: the one related to the human psyche. Psychologists, psychiatrists, educational psychologists, all are now in higher demand than ever before. We are entering a period of great uncertainty, and mental and emotional fragility is beginning to take hold. We're losing psychological control, and the diagnosis of "mental illness" is becoming ever more common.

Considering that this process is directly related to the human psyche, machines stand little chance of replacing an understanding of the human brain's complexity when it comes to helping people with psychological or psychiatric issues. We all have internal contradictions we face on a daily basis, and we can't always overcome them successfully. One could argue, as Lou Marinoff does, about whether it's appropriate to label people with certain self-control issues as either "patients" or "ill." It should also be noted that the fields of psychology and psychiatry are relatively recent, meaning that, until quite recently, the notion of "mental illness" didn't exist. Before such diagnoses became common, people routinely experienced similar difficulties in their daily lives, depending on their circumstances.

Mental illness can become normalized (and not necessarily considered a disease) if social circumstances dictate it. For some therapists, not all psychological diagnoses are of an actual illness. We mustn't forget that what has now come to be considered a mental illness is nothing more than a convention, an agreement made by a group of doctors who have concluded that it is appropriate for certain symptoms as well as their consequences to be considered a disease or defect.

For some philosophers, these mental illnesses shouldn't actually be considered as such, because before specific parameters were established, what is now being diagnosed and treated was, depending on the social context, considered entirely normal. Marinoff illustrates this in his discussion of post-traumatic stress disorder. What does it mean to suffer from this psychiatric condition? Simply put, it means the past still affects you in the present within a certain context. If, for example, some time ago, while walking down the street, you were bitten by a dog and had a panic attack, from that moment on you might develop a fear of dogs that now causes you to cross the street whenever you see one. In other words, being near a dog causes you discomfort or unease, something completely normal for people who haven't been able to overcome their fear of dogs. But what was once normal has now become an illness, and for some analysts, this step isn't always justified. Feeling bad is a part of life, but considering it a mental illness is another matter. So, we must tread cautiously when speaking about "mental illnesses" and know how to distinguish between a period of mourning after a partner has left us and a state of depression.

When it comes to the abundance of mental illnesses people suffer from in the twenty-first century, anxiety seems to carry the day. Anxiety is a mental illness that primarily affects the first world, or, rather, the developed Western world. That's how it's presented, and that's how we perceive it. One day, without really even knowing why, you relax. Your body, on the other hand, just when it's under the least amount of stress, decides to rebel against your mind. Your brain is seeking peace and quiet after a period of almost agonizing hyperactivity and is ready to disconnect, to enjoy a well-deserved mental vacation. But your body seems willing to disobey orders, and you gradually begin to feel a pang in your chest, an internal pinch that slowly grows, moving from uncomfortable to bothersome to genuinely painful. Your lungs can't seem to take in as much air as you need them to, and you become anxious. You try to inhale as much air as you can through your nose, hoping to inflate your chest, but when you do, there's a pain keeping you from doing so. You're short of breath, you're barely able to breathe, you're feeling a stabbing pain in your chest . . . you're having a panic attack. In my case, the short-term solution was IV muscle relaxers and a short, ten-day dose of antianxiety drugs. In the long term, though, the problem hasn't been quite so easily resolved. It has required the constant use of critical thinking to help me analyze the causes of anxiety and seek out realistic solutions tailored to my own personal circumstances. I had just turned thirty-one when this happened, and I haven't had another panic attack since then.

There are many factors that can trigger anxiety, but one of the most prominent is our self-imposed need for perfection. It's like we've been infected with "perfectionitis" without even having realized it. Byung-Chul Han, a South Korean philosopher living and teaching in Germany who unexpectedly became an internationally best-selling author (especially considering his most famous work is more of a treatise than a book), captured this idea brilliantly in his work—barely seventy pages in length—titled *The Burnout Society*. But in our case, the problem of being overly demanding of ourselves tends to creep in subconsciously and involuntarily, making it that much more difficult to eliminate. We expect too much of ourselves; we want to be as perfect as possible, and we want others to recognize this. We want to give our best in all aspects of life: to strive, to work, to be motivated, to dedicate ourselves to our responsibilities, and to surpass expectations. The question, then, is this: Where does this anxiety come from, this need to give everything we have to everything we do? Why do we feel impelled to achieve some supposed level of perfection? Wanting to improve as a person is normal. There's nothing wrong with wanting to make progress, with being active people looking to grow day by day. All this is fine, as long as the goal is to move closer to what the Greek philosophers referred to as "virtue." Today, being a virtuous person signifies having special abilities that set you apart, often when it comes to music (e.g., being a violin virtuoso) or athletics (e.g., being a soccer virtuoso). However, in its original, philosophical sense, virtue wasn't about having unique, innate abilities but rather personal training focused on developing one's personality.

For Aristotle, as well as many classical Greek thinkers, virtue is a habit acquired through practice, meaning anyone could acquire it. The opposite of virtue is vice. While virtue is the acquisition of good habits, vice is the acquisition of bad ones. If we listen to the great Aristotle, virtue was associated with knowledge not only of oneself but also of the circumstances surrounding the self, enabling us to know how to make decisions based on external and internal factors. And while it's somewhat reductionist, the doctrine of Aristotelian virtue is often summarized with the famous phrase that virtue is found in the middle ground, in the golden mean.

What did this sage philosopher—who, among many other admirable accomplishments, also served as the personal tutor to Alexander the Great—mean by this? At its core, it's about applying common sense, focusing on oneself, and avoiding the opinions and assessments of others. When undertaking an action or setting a goal, it's important to clearly consider the circumstances influencing them both. Achieving virtue is a slow yet steady process if pursued with the necessary calmness and conviction. What Aristotle was clear about—what we're all clear about—is that extremes are the antithesis of virtue, that the middle ground is the ideal guide for our lives, because excess and deficiency lie in the extremes. For example, in romantic relationships, the expectation is to maintain a fair balance between the love and passion one has for the other and for oneself. What would be unwise and unvirtuous would be to go to either of these two extremes; that is, to give yourself over body and soul to the other person with the sole aim of making them happy at all costs. That would be excessive. Or to focus entirely on yourself, casting your partner to the side while constantly demanding attention. This would be selfish and, therefore, a defect.

Being virtuous is directly linked to our responsibility. When people are looking to improve themselves, to increase their self-esteem, and therefore strive to overcome their vices and make positive progress, then they are on the right path toward a virtuous life. On the other hand, when they allow themselves to be overcome by vices and accept defeat without putting up a fight, then they are straying from that path. What's important about virtue is that it's entirely dependent on ourselves. It's a voluntary exercise that has nothing to do with other people's perceptions, and we often make the mistake of believing that we need society's recognition to be considered virtuous.

This mistake in valuing virtue is, among other things, what has led us to confuse virtue with virtuosity. This need for others to impose the label of "virtuous person" upon us is what often causes us to burn out in our attempts to meet the standards of success imposed by society. That's when we fall into the trap of being hyper-demanding with ourselves, of trying to be the best at everything: better workers, better parents, having better bodies, or being better partners or lovers. This pressure eventually takes its toll and activates the anxiety mechanism. We must learn to find our middle ground in every facet of our lives: as workers, fathers, mothers, husbands, wives, partners, children, athletes, friends, or whatever the case may be in order to achieve balance. Otherwise, antianxiety drugs will become part of our daily menu.

SEVENTEEN

Living for Success

Part of the responsibility for the anxiety we end up experiencing is determined by our notion of success. It's a concept linked almost exclusively to popular recognition and the world of work. The problem also arises when we find ourselves living for success. It's no wonder that mental disorders, depression, anxiety, and sadness eventually find ways to seep into our lives.

What does it mean to lead, have, or live a successful life? The answer is simpler than it might seem. Leading a successful life involves two important factors. The first, which we'll be analyzing later in the chapter dedicated to Epictetus (see chapter 27), is accepting fate's designs. In other words, knowing that what happens in your life isn't exclusively dependent on you, that there are countless uncontrollable and unforeseeable factors that are beyond your control, your calculations, or the plans you've set for yourself. Emotionally and rationally accepting these uncontrollable factors is of vital importance to leading a successful life.

Let's look at an example: I might be convinced that, for me, leading a successful life means finding the woman of my dreams, growing old together, being able to profoundly understand another person, and working hard to maintain a healthy relationship. But this involves the will of someone other than myself, a will that's difficult to control, and as such, when it comes to my model of success, it's an outside element. So, I have to be cognizant of the fact that I might not be able to construct that model if I base it on external factors over which I have little or no control.

Second, and perhaps this is the more difficult factor to put into practice, is participating in our own idea of success. We have an obligation to feel that we're the ones who have chosen for ourselves our model of a successful life through reflection instead of imitation, that we've been capable of analyzing ourselves, recognizing our shortcomings, our desires or virtues, and our flaws, that we know ourselves to the best of our abilities, and that we're constructing our life regardless of whether the rest of society agrees with or accepts us.

We are a highly suggestible species, and we live in a society in which everything is happening faster than ever. Innumerable wonderful stimuli accumulate around us like piles of snow, and we'd like to respond to all of them immediately. A sense of urgency takes over everything, leaving no room for reflection. We're easily entranced because, among other factors, society has accustomed us to a frenetically active pace, thereby making it easier for the System to seduce us with the prototypes for success that interest it.

It's a mistake to want the same thing as someone else simply because ill-considered envy has taken hold of us. We must be certain that the ambitions we have are truly our own—not borrowed or copied from another—and to not be guided by anything other than our own personal life analysis. Otherwise, we risk ending up like so many others who, after chasing or imitating someone else's model of success without ever having considered its suitability to themselves, wind up realizing that once they've achieved those standards of success, they feel neither happy nor fulfilled with their accomplishments.

SOCIAL RECOGNITION

The problem lies not in the desire to improve every aspect of one's life, but in the reason each person wants to do so. A reason that's rarely, if ever, realized. If it's done consciously and autonomously without waiting for external feedback, simply to feel better about oneself, about one's progress as a person, then we would be on the path of virtue. The problem arises when what we seek is the feedback from others with which to evaluate our virtue. At the moment this happens, we find ourselves living a misguided, poorly focused life, because we're placing the value of our actions—our virtue—in the hands of others, and it becomes an exercise in social acceptance rather than one of learning and improvement.

Take just a moment and think about what happens to us when we wait for recognition from others. Ultimately, what we're doing is lending power to their opinions, their points of view, and the ideas they have about us, about what we do, about who we are. And I'll emphasize this phrase again in case you read it too quickly: We give them power. When we wait for other people's recognition, we're granting them power over us that they wouldn't otherwise have. If you think long and hard about it, who in their right mind would consciously want to give another person power over them?

Without realizing it, we let ourselves be affected by other people's opinions because we lend them importance. And then there are the virtual social networks (Facebook, X, Instagram, etc.) where so many of the followers sharing their opinions are nothing more than digital acquaintances? It feels great to be recognized, to have others telling us that we're doing well, that we're good people, that we're on the right path, but if we believe them when things are looking good—if we're thrilled by the fact that other people are saying, posting, and thinking good things about us—then we've given those opinions an awful lot of power.

Strong, balanced people are those who understand that recognition from peers is good, but who don't get carried away by this kind of flattery. They don't value it as anything beyond a symbolic act because, if they did, they would be ceding power over themselves to many, many people. And what do you suppose would happen when those positive, encouraging opinions turned negative and harmful? Well, they would drag us down, but only because we allowed it to happen. By believing the good, positive comments about us—by allowing our personality to be defined by opinions, comments, and compliments—we've left ourselves exposed to the images others have created of who we are. We've sold ourselves out to someone else's judgment.

It always feels good to receive praise, but we can't let it affect the way we perceive ourselves. If praise affects us, then disparagement, contempt, or even simply being ignored will affect us just the same.

The primary need for recognition must come from within ourselves: knowing that we're doing things as best we can, that we're working to improve ourselves with every passing moment, that we're engaging in the act of critical thinking. Knowing our flaws as well as our strengths is necessary if we don't require any more recognition than what we grant to ourselves.

But since we're all humans, it can be quite difficult not to grant what, in Spanish, we call a *predicamento*—influence or authority, in English—to our loved ones. If we were to heed any sort of opinion or value-based judgment about us, it should come only from those people who make up our innermost circle of trust. The appreciation, affection, and even admiration of those we love will almost inevitably lead us to seek their approval and recognition. If we've managed to have a healthy and satisfying relationship with the people who surround us—if there is enough trust—we should pay attention to their perceptions of us because they won't be malicious or harmful but rather critical and constructive. They will be complementary perspectives of us, offering a new look at who we are. And it shouldn't hurt our feelings if the intention of these criticisms from within our close circle is to get us to change for the better or even simply to express how they see us from the point of view of people who also care about us. It's important that we consider, at least as a point of reflection, the possibility that these perspectives might well be useful contributions to the important process of our knowledge of self.

EIGHTEEN

Diogenes of Sinope: Thinking and Living in Coherence

Among the many philosophers we could mention regarding the importance of taking social recognition into account and seeing how this can affect a person's life, we'll talk about one who is unique: Diogenes of Sinope (400–323 BC). Diogenes was the son of a banker, Hicesias, who, it's been said, took advantage of his position and forged coins. He had to flee Sinope with his son, who had apparently helped in this counterfeiting process. Diogenes went into exile, ending up in Athens and becoming a disciple of Antisthenes. He began to lead a simple, frugal life, eventually earning the nickname of Diogenes the Dog for reasons we will explain shortly. He was quite the intriguing character, having gone from living in the lap of luxury in his native Sinope to being an exiled disciple without much financial support, achieving something of a material asceticism in which he needed almost nothing in order to live.

Another Diogenes, Diogenes Laërtius, a writer who compiled many of the ancient historiographical sources on the philosophers of that era in a book titled *The Lives and Opinions of Eminent Philosophers*, presents him as a person who, little by little, through observing the lives of others and the things taking place around them, developed a model in which life and thought merged, thus turning the lack of need into a virtue. He gained fame and admiration that spread beyond Athens throughout all of Greece, and even when Alexander the Great came to meet him, telling him that he would grant him anything he asked, Diogenes simply asked him to step aside because he was blocking the sunlight. This is the attitude of a true cynic: Someone who was able to demonstrate to the most powerful man in the world that he possessed nothing of value that could possibly interest him, and that the only thing he does value—the sun—is beyond the reach of even Alexander the Great.

It's been said that, by watching a mouse roam freely, coming and going, unconcerned by anything, he realized that this must be one of life's goals. When it was time to sleep, he would ball up his own clothing to use as a pillow, and any old place could serve quite well as a bed. In fact, he is thought to have said that the Echo Stoa of Zeus had been decorated and adorned just so that he could live under it. He needed fewer and fewer material things; he was like an Athenian vagabond with no real luggage other than a basin and a walking stick, the latter necessary to ward off undesirables.

Of the many surviving anecdotes that have managed to reach us, the most enduring one of all is that he lived in a *pithos*—often translated as a "jar," "tub," or "barrel"—a story that seems to be corroborated by another: After having earned the intellectual respect of his peers, a young man shattered the *pithos* in which he liked to rest. The citizenry beat the young man and gave Diogenes a new jar so he could once again take up his abode there.

He was characterized as having what we might call "a sharp tongue," and for never holding anything back. He was critical of everyone: Euclid's school, Platonic teachings, Dionysian festivals . . . and in doing so, he mocked the academicism of many. Plato famously defined man as a "a featherless biped," and Diogenes took advantage of the opportunity to pluck the feathers from a chicken and hold it up before Plato's school and cried, "Behold: a man!"

He was enslaved at one point, but his arrogance and contempt for the concerns of men he considered vile and inferior led him to instruct the auctioneer selling the slaves to loudly ask the assembled bidders if anyone would like to purchase a master, referring to himself. He questioned the theories of the great schools of thought and had the occasional intellectual clash with the great Plato himself.

He laughed at the absurdity of humankind, and while the following example can't be definitively attributed to him, it nonetheless aligns with his philosophy of life. It can be argued that most human beings are just a finger's width away from crazy. If someone walks down the street extending their middle finger into the air, essentially flipping everyone off, people will think that person is crazy. But if you do the same thing with your index finger, they'll think the exact opposite.

What almost everyone agrees on is Diogenes's incredible ability to need virtually nothing, to ignore material goods. He was invited to feasts offering the most lavish of delicacies, yet Diogenes boasted of needing nothing, mocking those who did. He preferred to see himself as a dog, a dog that everyone praises yet no one wants to be around or take out for a hunt. His goal was to live as rudimentary a life as possible. It's also been said that he once observed a child drinking from a fountain using his own hands as a bowl. Seeing this, he took out his basin, removed the cup he used for drinking and tossed it aside, asserting that the child's hands surpassed him in terms of simplicity.

In short, we can say that Diogenes was someone who managed to merge thought and life in a truly exemplary manner. He lived according to the results and conclusions of his philosophy. To put it another way, he achieved something tremendously difficult for any person, ancient or modern: consistency. He had a well-developed and finely honed critical mindset, and he managed to put his philosophy of life into practice, becoming a touchstone for thought and establishing a lifestyle admired by many of his fellow citizens. This admiration comes not only from flipping that switch but also from having the determination to act based on the conclusions of his thinking, avoiding contradictions between word and deed and ensuring that his form of thinking didn't deviate from his way of life. When we realize the difficulty of actually doing something like this—when we encounter a figure like Diogenes—we have no choice but to give him the recognition he so richly deserves.

CYNICS: CRITICAL THINKING FOR SOCIAL CONVENTIONS

It certainly wouldn't hurt to have the same gift for observation of such a unique thinker, especially when it comes to the realization that, as he himself argued, the important things in life are worth very little when it comes to material or monetary value. Meanwhile, the things that tend to cost a lot aren't always that important.

There's a lesson here for our current age of overabundance, one that would be wise to put into practice: achieving an austere sense of independence, both materially and socially. Not needing or depending on anyone or anything—especially social recognition—greatly facilitates the path to self-sufficiency.

The ultimate goal, if we're to learn something practical from this unique man, is to lead as simple a life as possible. The anecdote of the boy using his hands to drink from a fountain is the perfect example of what we're talking about. And while we're not about to start throwing away all our personal possessions, it might be wise to evaluate the relative importance they ought to have in our lives.

Another valuable lesson we can draw from his life is the importance of focusing our existence on real and important things that don't cost us any more time than what's necessary. He laughed at those who spent their days debating irrelevant things; for example, when he came across people arguing that motion didn't exist, he simply got up and walked away. And when he encountered others discussing the stars, he would ask them, "When did you descend from the heavens?" These retorts are laden with irony and cynicism—it could be no other way from the father of cynicism himself—and are meant to show us how often we devote time and energy to truly insubstantial things.

He reproached people for worrying about their dreams while not caring about what was happening to them while awake. Or for those who spent their days entertaining themselves with dreamlike fantasies instead of reality. Today we make a similar mistake whenever we tell someone to "dream big," to get excited about a possibility and set it up as something to aim for instead of encouraging them to focus on their immediate reality. We're living in the empire of emotions, and dreaming creates illusions that make us feel good, which is why motivational speakers and emotional trainers (or "life coaches") continue to multiply. But rather than training us in and on reality, they seek simply to enhance our emotional fantasies.

When it comes to Diogenes, instead of philosophical essays, we have stories about his life, his sayings, his phrases, and the attitude he took with events. But each of these anecdotes contains a sliver of behavioral advice that, as we're seeing, can still be very useful to us in these modern times. You don't have to be some sagacious philosopher who writes unreadable treatises and books to learn to think well. It's enough to keep the critical thinking switch flipped on to face everyday things, the events and anecdotes that encompass our daily lives.

One of the most famous—or perhaps infamous—anecdotes has to do with masturbation. It's been said that, on one occasion, he did so in public, for which he was harshly reprimanded. He was accused of acting like a dog, and it wasn't the first time. During a banquet, people are said to have thrown bones on the ground for him to eat, but instead he sniffed them and urinated on them, just as a dog might do. Regarding masturbation, Diogenes argued that there ought to be a similar mechanism, such that rubbing one's belly would make hunger disappear. What could Diogenes possibly mean by this comparison? Well, it's something that often goes overlooked: the naturalness with which we should address sexual matters in our lives. Diogenes rejected social conventions and had little regard for other schools of thought of the time, because both accepted customs as valid without regard for whatever inherent truth they contained.

The way a society chooses to approach the topic of sex goes a long way to defining its collective taboos. Sex, as Diogenes tried to tell us, is completely natural; it's a physical need, just like food. If everyone could satisfy their hunger by rubbing their stomach, wouldn't we be doing that in public? In other words, if we know how to calm our sexual appetite without anyone else's involvement, why hide that from public life? It's still great advice today to consider topics related to sexuality as naturally as possible. We still have a lot to learn in this respect. Talking openly about penises, vaginas, breasts, ejaculation, periods, orgasms, the G-spot—it's still difficult, especially when it comes to sex education. Reevaluating our attitudes and behaviors on the subject wouldn't be a bad idea.

But perhaps the most remarkable thing about this figure is his utter disregard for social recognition. In fact, it's been said that he would walk the streets of Athens carrying a lantern in the middle of the day shouting, "I'm looking for a man." But Diogenes was always honest and he lived as he preached without any need for approval from his peers. The odd thing about this case—which is also one of the primary lessons we can apply to ourselves—is that despite it all, as we've seen, he still gained the recognition of his fellow citizens and ended up in the history books. Which is to say, acknowledgment shouldn't be the goal of any of the paths through life we undertake because, among other things, it's not up to oneself. You can never control what others consider important or worthy of admiration. If we seek fame, popularity, or celebrity, we're simply missing the point, because we can't control what others choose to admire or not. Being honest with yourself, being confident in your knowledge and abilities, and showing perseverance and determination are the best ways to be accepted. If recognition comes later, then one must know how to handle it with the same naturalness and importance as we did before it arrived.

Before moving on, I want to acknowledge one of most interesting details from this whole process: Diogenes questioned the social conventions and cultural aspects of his time, and although he was on the receiving end of some beatings, hair-pulling, spitting, and contempt from a few Athenians, it was nonetheless Alexander the Great who expressed his admiration for him, even going so far as to say that if he weren't who he was, he would have wanted to be Diogenes. To put it another way, instead of generating rejection and antipathy, he garnered respect thanks to the fact that he exercised constructive criticism of the society of his time and was always consistent in what he defended. He didn't devote himself to ranting and raving about everyone and everything—something that seems to be quite common today—but he always argued and demonstrated that another way of approaching life was possible.

ANTIPATHY

There are many reasons why people feel the need for the recognition of others to feel good or confident in themselves and what they do. Here we'll try to clarify some of them in order to see, once analyzed, whether we identify with any of them. Being accepted is one thing, while being recognized is another. And it's not a good idea to mix the two. Feeling accepted is almost necessary to feel human . . . to know that you're part of a group, a community, a society, a planet.

When Aristotle attempts to define humankind, he refers to our species as a "political animal" in need of a society. It's as if it were embedded in our DNA. When we're born, we're one of the most defenseless creatures on Earth. We require a lengthy process or nurturing and maturation—longer than almost any other species of animal—which means we depend on others in order to develop and grow. If, in biological terms, we need others so we can become what we are, then the social process is no different. The other—our fellow human—teaches us how to be part of the group, the whole. As Aristotle pointed out, first the family, then the tribe, later the cities . . . yet always groups, always collectives. Therefore, if we need others in both the biological and cultural sense, it's only natural that we feel accepted by the different groups we encounter throughout life.

Earning the recognition of others, though, is more complicated. They may accept you as part of the group, appreciate you, even value you—that is, they see you as adding something positive to the group—but that's not the same. Given that we're accepted into different social groups to varying degrees depending on how close-knit the group is, recognition tends to be "necessary" for the vast majority of us. In a perfect world, we wouldn't need it—at the very least, we wouldn't have to depend on it as a guiding principle of our lives—and yet it's still true that we need our closest, dearest, and most admired people to show us some degree of recognition. And, indeed, this recognition is important as long as it's honest, as long as we've established and maintained channels of trust in our relationships that are clear and transparent enough for their opinions to carry value.

In principle, we need recognition to strengthen our personality as we grow and evolve. As with any educational process, it's important to have guides and mentors who possess the requisite frankness to tell us what we're doing well and where we can improve. When we're in a process of growth and maturation, it's essential that, at certain moments and in certain matters, we feel that we're receiving a positive evaluation from others. There is nothing more damaging to the education of a well-balanced person and the development of that person's happiness than having low self-esteem. This is often the result of never having received sufficient recognition from the people in our close-knit circles of life, from the people we considered most essential during the key stages of our personal development. Thus, as we make decisions and move through those critical, formative stages, being certain that the recognition we're receiving is sincere, honest, and positive is vital when it comes to forging a calm, confident personality.

Apart from self-esteem, social acceptance, along with recognition, is important to avoid what we might call antipathy. It comes from the Latin word *antipathia*, which in turn comes from the Greek *antĭpátheiă*. *Anti*, meaning "against" or "negation," and *pathos*, meaning "emotion" or "feeling," so the most common semantic meaning would be the "opposition of feelings," which in our context means, according to the *Oxford English Dictionary*: "Natural or intrinsic contrariety or incompatibility, real or supposed, between certain things, animals, etc., by virtue of which they repel, resist, or adversely affect one another; an instance of this. Opposed to sympathy."

It's a sort of unpopularity in the eyes of one's peers. Acceptance doesn't necessarily imply a moral judgment about a person, but recognition tends to have a higher value because it means we're not only accepted but also positively valued.

To be recognized, all we need to do is adapt to the social conventions of the group, follow the habits and customs of the culture, or, at the very least, don't contradict them. For our ancestors, customs were more rigid, more strict; they were clearly marked by social and historical circumstances, social class, education, place of birth. The boundaries were all clearly defined, so to avoid reaching the level of antipathy, one had to act within those boundaries. If, on the one hand, everything was clear and the consequences of crossing these boundaries could be predicted easily and apparently, then on the other, those same inflexible boundaries caused great dissatisfaction when it came to the pursuit of happiness.

Fortunately for us, these boundaries have become more flexible and in some cases have even been broken. However, other boundaries have become personalized. With the rise of individualism, boundaries are not so much a social convention, an imperative imposed from the outside, and instead are presented as a construct of the individual. In an era of hypermodernity, boundaries are hyper-individualistic. While in the past it was easier to know what the boundaries were, which therefore made social acceptance and support more accessible to anyone, now, in the midst of globalization, as boundaries are beginning to diversify, it's much more complicated to gain recognition from others. This is mainly due to the fact that when an individual sets his or her own boundaries, there are as many boundaries as there are individuals, and social conventions become so stretched, so expansive, that almost every type of person can be accommodated.

There is a tiny bit of common ground, just a few foundational bases upon which we all operate in society, but other than that, it's difficult to achieve recognition from others when everyone has their own perspective on the process. What is admirable to some may be reprehensible to others; what some consider an art—bullfighting, for example—is to others a criminal act. And with easy and immediate access to social media, it's astonishing just how quickly we can find outpourings of support and condemnation for any idea being presented.

Antipathy has dual connotations. On the one hand, it's a sign of notoriety, since you're able to stand out in a negative way, having become noticeable to a large number of people who find you disagreeable or unlikable. In this open and flexible society where interpretation has been expanded to include multiple perspectives, being disliked by others means that they've at least taken the trouble to get to know you or learn something about you. It means you've surpassed a certain level of indifference and anonymity, which, considering our current times, is no small feat. But on the other hand, it generates nearly irrevocable rejection from those who consider you disagreeable, because you've challenged certain social conventions of people who've drawn their own insurmountable boundaries that you've dared to traverse. What's essential and nonnegotiable for some people is absurd and trivial for others.

NINETEEN

The Kingdom of Manichaeanism

We'll have to be quite careful with this one. In this historical moment, where there appears to be more flexibility and openness than ever before, we still find many people anchored within an inflexible system of thought in which they feel safe from social indeterminism, from the relaxing of boundaries we're talking about. These are the radical Manichaeans who understand the world in binary terms, who only conceive of reality in two ways. In their eyes, you're either with me or against me—you're one of us or you aren't. This way of thinking, which demands that you take one position or its opposite, often suffers from what I call "the fallacy of denial." This fallacy usually occurs when people interpret silence or the lack of a response to two opposing alternatives as a denial. And I use the word "interpret" because it's the radical Manichaeans who reject prudence, modesty, or simple indifference as valid ways of seeing things.

And while this may sound awkward, I'll use a personal example to illustrate what I'm talking about here. When I published the book *From Plato to Batman*, I participated in some interviews with journalists who criticized me for not including more female philosophers or superheroines. One even suggested a certain sexist and patriarchal bias, both in the characters I'd selected and the language I'd used. I must say that, when I was writing it, the methodology was more about focusing research and disseminating the topics to be discussed than the people or superheroes associated with them. That is, I didn't pay attention to the gender of the person—real or fictional—I was using to support my theories on education.

Regrettably, women haven't played a prominent role in the history of philosophy: A role that, fortunately, we are now beginning to reclaim and assign the importance it deserves. In comics, things seem to have been quite similar. Historically, superheroes were mostly men. So, in my selection process, I did include women like Mary Shelley and superheroines like Wonder Woman, but they were outnumbered by male philosophers and superheroes. The thought of meeting quotas never entered my mind, and much to my surprise, I was criticized for this potentially sexist tendency that perpetuated the myth of patriarchy. That's when I brought up the fallacy of denial, which simply means that just because something isn't mentioned or considered doesn't mean that the opposite view is being promoted. There are countless reasons why something might have gone unnoticed or not been taken into account, but from these factors—and there may be many—one cannot simply infer that you're against it. These critics made an illegitimate leap from absence to negation, and it activates the "you're either with me or against me" mechanism. On a social level, these are the people who are the most intransigent and dangerous people.

What's interesting is that we all carry a bit of this Manichaeanism in us, depending on the topic, oftentimes politics, religion, or economics. We might tend to be tolerant, lenient, flexible when it comes to other subjects that we scarcely acknowledge or pay attention to because we don't consider them important or necessary. But when it comes to a topic we're passionate about or interested in, that's precisely where we seek out recognition and where antipathy is generated. It's where we want others to take us and our ideas into consideration, and it's also where we're most inclined to show our disdain and disregard for others.

This is why it's important to know how to assess the person with whom we're interacting if we want to avoid creating a sense of antipathy. If we do this well enough, we can turn antipathy into appreciation. If we pay attention to the other person's attitudes, their context and culture, their way of formulating thoughts and expressing themselves—and if we're intelligent enough ourselves—we might just turn what could have been animosity into admiration.

To offer an example, if we are against the institution of marriage, and we meet a newlywed couple, launching into a tirade against eternal love and lifelong commitment until death do us part would be foolhardy, having put the person you're speaking with on the defensive from the very beginning. But on the other hand, we can turn to a well-known philosophical method that can help us engage in intelligent dialogue without directly attacking our peers' beliefs, opinions, or points of view. This, which we will examine in the next chapter, is known as the maieutic method.

SOCRATES: WAYS OF LIVING

Socrates is an Athenian thinker historically recognized by his peers, especially the city's younger people, a generation that included none other than Plato himself, who was Socrates's disciple and possibly the most influential philosopher in the history of thought. Much has been written about Socrates, and yet nothing remains that was written by his own hand, likely because he could barely write. His teachings have been passed down to us through his students, followers, and the historians who learned of him. Socrates was known as "The Ugly One" due to his physical appearance, but he was also referred to as "The Wasp" because it's been said he had a rather annoying stinger and was constantly pricking people. But this sting of his was nothing more than his way of forcing people, through questioning, to reflect for themselves on what they say or think, to dig down beneath the superficial layer. So much so, in fact, that it's also been said that on more than one occasion, during a heated debate, he would end up getting his hair pulled, his head smacked, or punched in the face, and that his most irascible opponents ended up despising and mocking him, something he was never affected by.

He was born in Athens around 469 BC and died in 399 BC. His father is believed to have been a sculptor and his mother a housewife who worked as a midwife when necessary. He came from a middle-class family. During his formative years, he followed the teachings of the philosopher Archelaus, who in turn was a disciple of Anaxagoras. Not much is known about Archelaus's teachings, but from the little we can say, he maintained that justice and injustice do not stem from nature itself, but are, rather, social conventions that originate in the law. One of the most important researchers and sources of ancient Greek history, Diogenes Laërtius, whom we've already mentioned, declares in his book *The Lives and Opinions of Eminent Philosophers* that Archelaus was the thinker who "imported the study of natural philosophy from Ionia to Athens." Be that as it may, what seems clear is that he was the one who sparked Socrates's curiosity in philosophy, particularly when it came to questions of morality. But, according to Diogenes, what's most interesting about this thinker is that "he, likewise, was the first person who conversed about human life; and was also the first philosopher who was condemned to death and executed."

Just about all historians agree that Socrates had a gift for rhetoric and public speaking, and that he was also one of the first philosophers to abandon the prevailing trend of the time: focusing on understanding nature, the cosmos, and the physical origins of the world. Instead, he devoted his research and time to moral and political issues. But among this thinker's peculiarities, what's interesting for our purposes is to highlight the fact that he attempted to reflect on moral issues in his city's public spaces. He philosophized in workshops and in the public square; he had no qualms about speaking to anyone, whether a renowned Athenian general, politician, sculptor, or carpenter.

His lack of snobbery when it came to engaging equally with people of diverse occupations and social classes demonstrated an open-mindedness that people of the era weren't expecting. His fame spread throughout Greece, and it's been said that he lived a very unfettered life, caring little about food or footwear, considering he often strolled barefoot about the Agora with dirty feet and a fetid tunic. It's no wonder he had a certain reputation for being a bit malodorous. But he also had what, today, we call "charisma": He had an acutely compelling personality, and many young Athenians—including the children of Athens's political elite—fell in love with this thinker's words and teachings.

Socrates's problems didn't arise solely from his sharp tongue or his wasplike nature. According to Diogenes, the problems began when Chaerephon, a disciple who had visited the Oracle of Delphi to have his future foretold, brought back to Athens the Oracle's famous response: that Socrates was the wisest man in all Greece. The Greeks held the Oracle in high regard, so what it prophesized quickly became *vox populi*. And this particular verdict regarding Socrates earned him a great deal of envy among his peers. How could it be that a ragged, dirty, ugly, smelly, intellectual annoyance with no social standing, barely any money, and an ostentatiously simple life be considered the wisest Greek alive?

His fame—the recognition of his wisdom—was perhaps the beginning of what would ultimately become his death sentence. This, coupled with the fact that, according to some of Plato's dialogues, *Meno* among them, Socrates enjoyed exposing the powerful to show the only true power was that of knowledge. Thus, between the envy provoked by his fame as the wisest man in Greece and the chagrin of those who were revealed as ignorant, he found himself accused of corrupting the Athenian youth and of being impious toward the gods. The accusation of corrupting the youth was based on the fact that some of his younger followers had participated in the Thirty Tyrants dictatorship, and Socrates was suspected of having been the instigator by means of corrupting their minds. Socrates justified himself by saying he wasn't responsible for other people's actions, but this argument was of little avail. In addition to this, the teacher displayed a bit of arrogance when facing his accusers in court. After hearing the charges and the request of accusers for the death sentence, the usual course of action would be for the accused to show remorse and either have his sentence reduced or request a life in exile. Instead, Socrates not only asked the jury to allow him to continue his activities, he proposed the State reward him with a palace and an annuity for having educated the Athenian youth free of charge for his entire life. Predictably, when faced with such audacity, those judging him had little choice but to sentence him to death.

Socrates was always particularly interested in teaching people how to think properly—or, at least, how to properly question things—and he did so with anyone who would listen. To attain knowledge, it's essential to know how to ask questions, which is why he believed that asking questions was the first step on the path toward discernment. He was also convinced that knowledge was accessible to the vast majority of people and that one can approach the truth if one seeks it.

He clashed with another group of philosophers of the time: the Sophists, who didn't believe any truth existed other than that which was relative to the individual and the context of each individual. Sophists were relativists when it came to defending one truth or its opposite: Everything depended on the interests and circumstances of the moment. Like Socrates, they were excellent orators. Unlike him, though, they tended to take advantage of their skills and traveled from city to city teaching and indoctrinating anyone willing to pay for it.

In short, we could say that Sophists earned a living from their teachings, like educators offering instruction on subjects that interested people wanted to know more about. They were among the first thinkers to professionalize their knowledge and profit from it. They had the requisite need—not many came from the ranks of the wealthy, as most philosophers at the time did—and ability to adapt their talents and teachings wherever they went and managed to live a decent life. Unlike Socrates, they were skeptical about the existence of absolute truth and leaned more toward relativism. Socrates branded them as charlatans and found this self-interested and materialistic relativism rooted in the monetization of their teachings to be quite dangerous for anyone's education. In fact, for Socrates, if there were no valid truth—if anything goes—then we would be morally corrupting our youth. Ironically, this was the very same charge that would later be levied against him. It's been said that the speech accusing him of being impious and corrupting the youth was written by the Sophist Polycrates, achieving the desired effect before the court, though this isn't entirely clear in the historical records.

What everyone does seem to agree on is the mutual antipathy between Socrates and the practitioners of Sophism. What happened to Socrates—being loathed, considered suspicious, even earning him the hatred of those we question, criticize, or challenge—could happen to any of us. Unpopularity begins with rejection. Socrates had left a lot of powerful people seeing red by encouraging people to think for themselves, to question issues deeply embedded in the bedrock of popular belief such as the existence of the gods or the legitimacy of those in power. Inciting people—especially young people from well-to-do families in Athens at the time—to question their philosophy of life ended up garnering him powerful enemies who managed to get rid of him because they considered him a subversive element threatening the stability and control of the city, control exercised by the powerful with an almost unquestioned authority.

Rethinking social conventions, questioning and investigating them, being able to think about them critically, effectively, and functionally will always be a dangerous and disruptive element in the eyes of the elite. When those who wield authority and control over a society detect that someone has gained enough influence to make others question where their power comes from, whether it's legitimate for them to hold so much power, whether it's fair for them to be in possession of that power, whether something could be done to change the social situation in which they live . . . they will then deploy every instrument of coercion and constraint they have in order to eliminate the worst of all threats, the most dangerous weapon of mass destruction that exists in society: free and critical thinking.

MAIEUTICS: TRICKERY VERSUS ANTIPATHY

There is, however, a certain coincidence in the way Socrates oriented his teachings, and he has gone down in history not only as Plato's teacher but also as the greatest exponent of a philosophical method known as maieutics. Maieutics comes from the classical Greek and means "to give birth." The story is well-known: Socrates's mother was a midwife: She helped bring new life into the world. Socrates chose a working method not unlike that of his mother: His job was to help people give birth to their own ideas.

It's a method conducive to both introspection and analysis, and it's quite useful to better understand where our ideas and beliefs come from, whether they have a solid foundation, or if, on the contrary, we've allowed ourselves to be guided by popular sayings, superstitions, and pseudo-truths. At its core, the method consists of asking questions about the knowledge we believe we possess or seek to achieve. Maieutics, then, is a material technique that helps give birth to the truth.

Maieutics doesn't uncover the truth. After all, it is the patient who must give birth; the midwife can only help and facilitate. Therefore, the search for truth is induced through questions whose purpose is for the subject to produce knowledge for themselves. It's a means of discussion with a pedagogical aim of bringing the other person as close as possible to the truth, or at least to be able to shed some false beliefs.

It's actually not all that difficult to put into practice, and it's an excellent critical thinking exercise for those who want to advance their knowledge. First, choose any sort of idea, thought, or statement that's accepted broadly enough to be considered common sense. Then, start by assuming that this thought (idea, reflection, statement) is false and search for an example, context, or situation in which that thought doesn't hold true. If we're able to find this first exception, the deduction is, then, that what initially seemed like common sense or an obvious truth is no longer so, and therefore we must accept the exception as part of the definition, thereby refining our knowledge. But if we're able to encounter more examples, we will then be forced to redefine what we previously considered obvious. In this way, we inch closer to the truth by progressively discarding whatever this idea/principle/statement is not. It's a kind of approximation by negation.

Many of Plato's dialogues feature his teacher Socrates, and they offer examples of how this methodology is used. Each dialogue generally begins with a discussion point, whether it's love, friendship, justice, art, and so on. There's always someone who's clear about what each topic means, someone who claims to know what friendship is, who understands love well, who believes they possess the criteria for handing down judgments. Socrates, then, using the answers or arguments offered by his conversational partner, begins asking questions that compel the other person to come up with arguments that defend the ideas—targeted, propulsive questions fired through the lens of critical thinking. The intent of this process is to lead this person—who initially had complete confidence in the ideas—to gradually realize that many of them lack the solid, rational foundations they were thought to have. This, in turn, provokes doubt, which itself leads to a change in thinking, helping them move forward along the path toward truth, all the while demonstrating that the critical thinking switch must always remain engaged.

Maieutics can be quite useful when it comes to combating antipathy and awakening a sense of recognition among our peers. Generally speaking, expressing opinions contrary to those held by another person—taking a stand against the customs and beliefs of someone who has spent an entire life transforming these beliefs into ideas, into "knowledge"—is counterproductive and unpopular. It leads to misunderstanding and, in the worst cases, ends in antipathy, particularly because the other person often feels attacked, because they interpret the antithesis as a contradiction, not a stimulation. Even acceptance can be a rather difficult experience. But if we use maieutics, we might just be able to reverse a potentially hostile situation into one of recognition. Instead of offering counterarguments and trying to make someone accept an opposing idea, regardless of how much evidence you present, it's more effective if the other person arrives at your intended point on his or her own. It's far more efficient for people to reach their truth without confrontation. To do that, we replace the dialectical dispute with a process of inquiry, of questioning what the other person believes, thinks, or knows.

Imagine that your children (friends, partners, etc.) have an idea that stems from a common misconception, and you want to make them realize that they're mistaken. You know they're wrong, and you have an argument with which to refute them. Well, there are two options: Either you confront their truth, which is so deeply rooted that it is next to impossible to extract with simple counterargument, or you pursue another strategy. In this first case, especially if the others tend to get carried away by emotional arguments, it will be quite difficult to get them to alter their stance through a dialectical battle. Very often, culture, education, and context have led people to internalize their beliefs and turn them into ideas, making it that much harder for them to let those ideas go. If you don't believe it, just try getting teenagers to change their mind about their friends.

The other option we have is to use maieutics intelligently and provoke doubts about their ideas through guided, targeted questioning. Ask them to explain where their ideas come from, what justifications they might have for them, who taught them, or how they learned them. Question the legitimacy of their sources. Ultimately, it's much more productive as well as effective to sow the seeds of doubt through questions than it is to try to rip out mistaken ideas by the root.

There's a Spanish saying, "Nobody learns from other people's mistakes," and there's a lot of truth in those words. We have to get people to realize for themselves that they've taken beliefs and converted them into ideas, that they've given an epistemological status they didn't have before. They have to feel that we're genuinely interested in their ideas, that we want to know more about them, that we're asking thoughtful questions to better understand them, and that those questions reflect our unresolved curiosity. Then, in addition to guiding others along their journey toward truth, we will have also earned their appreciation for having helped them through this process of enlightenment while avoiding the potential hostility direct confrontation might have provoked. Instead of earning the antipathy of others in an attempt to oppose their ideas, beliefs, customs, and so on, it's far more helpful to present ourselves as people who want to know, who are curious about the origins of these ideas, who are asking the kinds of questions that prompt others to think of accurate, convincing answers. By knowing how to use maieutics appropriately, we can transform antipathy into admiration and respect.

TWENTY

Alain de Botton: Snobbery and the Obsession with Labeling

One of the problems that calls most urgently for flipping the critical thinking switch is the way we deal with social status on a daily basis. Globalization has brought wonderful diversity in terms of offering a vast array of options from which to choose a lifestyle in which each and every one of us can feel comfortable. The problem arises when, once we've found our optimal lifestyle, we want others to recognize it as such and hold it in high esteem. We want, we long, for our chosen lifestyle to attain an impressive social status in the eyes of others. Problems arise from this self-imposed need for recognition and admiration, a need that demonstrates the low value and lack of self-esteem we ascribe to our own life project, to our own philosophy, since we need the approval of others in order to feel satisfied.

I remember a conversation with a friend who works at a high-end car dealership in Córdoba. I had asked her about the type of customer who usually walked into their showroom, and among the many who had bought luxury vehicles, we focused on a peculiar type of customer they'd labeled by the postal code in which they lived, known as the 14012s. These were customers who lived in the wealthy part of the city, but they themselves weren't quite as well-off as they seemed. They wanted to buy an expensive car, and yet they were the only ones who sought out the longest possible financing—ten-year installments—and barely spent anything on upgrades. Under no circumstances were they going to lose the appearance of social status, because for them the image they outwardly projected was paramount. These sorts of people are commonly known as "snobs."

Alain de Botton has a definition of a snob that's quite appropriate for our times: "A snob is someone who takes a small part of you and uses that to create a complete vision of who you are. That's snobbery." That one small part is most commonly associated with your job or your apparent social status. Second, they will often judge you by other things such as the clothes you wear, the car you drive, where you go on vacation, or the school your children attend.

Of all the snobbery we might come across, the one that seems most deeply rooted is occupational snobbery associated with social status. If you don't believe it, try it for yourself: The next time you introduce yourself to a stranger, say that you're a lawyer, a judge, or a surgeon, and you'll see how the consideration afforded your words and the attitudes of those with whom you're speaking are different from what they would be when we're introducing ourselves as plumbers, bricklayers, or house painters. For many people, the work you perform determines not only your rank in the social hierarchy but also—and even worse—the type of person you are.

It does happen, on occasion, that when someone finds out that you're a philosopher, they seem to expect every sentence you utter to be some sort of brilliant aphorism that leaves them temporarily stunned. Naturally, after conversing with me for a bit, they end up disappointed, saying something along the lines of, "Well, for someone who does philosophy, you seem pretty normal." This example, which I've experienced firsthand on more than one occasion, serves to illustrate the tremendous importance that professional appearances often have when it comes to labeling and defining a person. It's not so common to ask others if they're married, if they have any kids, how they spend their free time, if they like movies, if they're happy. The only question that seems to matter is: "What do you do?"

Defining someone by their profession is not only first-class snobbery, but it also conditions the way in which someone sees themselves when it comes to self-evaluation. This type of snobbery, limited to the world of work, is focused on something as reductionist yet as impactful to today's society as accomplishments. In other words, a snob judges others by their professional achievements and material possessions. Personality takes a backseat.

To avoid this kind of snobbery, the best thing we can do is to not be exclusively interested in the professional achievements of the people we know . . . at least not initially. Talking shop is common among acquaintances, and while it can take up a significant portion of our time, it would be much better in terms of our mental health and our social relationships to focus more on the personal aspects of others as well as ourselves rather than professional achievements and goals. Generally, the love that parents have for their children is the best example of anti-snobbery. These are the people who know you better than anyone, who are aware of your flaws and virtues alike, who accept you without the need to evaluate every move you make. They don't value you based on your job, your partner, or your social status. They're the exact opposite of a snob: They love you unconditionally.

Being a snob means making a sweeping judgment based on a single statistical item, drawing generalized conclusions using just a few data points as indicators. Generally speaking, we can't help but label and categorize people because it gives us a sense of well-being. But we have to remember that people cannot be reduced to that one (or those few) facts we know about them.

It's important that we ease up on our obsession with labeling and pigeonholing people. If we want to be more fair in our judgments of others, we must keep the mental boxes into which we assign people open and try to understand the immense complexity of what it means to know and understand others. And, of course, when we reduce this understanding to a few bits of data and then create a complete portrait of the person from them, we aren't being fair to each individual's reality.

TWENTY-ONE

Martin Luther and the American Dream: Work as a Swindle

Along with globalization, messages about personal development and happiness are increasingly associated with the world of work, and as such, the emotional spectrum of life has expanded into a sector that had previously seen little if any emotional affiliation: the world of work. All of a sudden, we have exponentially increased the importance of emotional life by introducing it into the workplace. Now we're expected to be happy from the moment we wake up until the minute we lay down to sleep. In the past, a smile and a sense of relief were reserved for coming home from work and seeing the light in your child's eyes, when you were having dinner with your partner and talking about what an exhausting day it was, or when you're lying on the couch waiting for the latest episode of your favorite TV series to begin. The realization of this joy was limited to your personal life, to your free, leisurely time. It was only a privileged few who had the opportunity to turn their hobbies into work.

But ever since we've been sold on the message that we must seek, find, and follow our passion, explore and live our calling

(Sir Ken Robinson's TED Talks deserve special attention here), we're burdened with the heavy load of expanding happiness, even into the workplace. This has been one of the most damaging messages for human beings' emotional evolution. This need to be happy twenty-four hours a day—especially at work—is causing anxiety and dissatisfaction.

Until now, work has served to earn money, and money is essential for life. Work is important because it is the primary means by which we live, by which our vital needs are covered, and depending on the situation, by which we satisfy our desires as well. The history of philosophy is clear when it states that the first thing to do is ensure basic needs; after that, one could begin to think. The exact phrase is attributed to the English philosopher Thomas Hobbes, but it was already known in classical Greek and Roman times: *Primun vivere deinde phisophari* (not exactly a literal translation, but "Live first, then philosophize"). One simply cannot practice philosophy without meeting one's basic needs. For some of the most illustrious classical Greek thinkers such as Aristotle, philosophy arose from leisure; that is, from having enough free time to think about things other than how I'm going to put some food on the table, where I'm going to sleep tonight, or how I'm going to provide for my children. In fact, for this student of Plato who opened his own school, the Lyceum, intellectual life was only accessible to people in good economic standing who could afford to enjoy freedom. He considered those who had to earn a living to be a kind of slave as opposed to a free person, because they were compelled to work out of necessity.

But, here in the twenty-first century, work has taken a significant turn, especially with regard to the importance placed on personal development. People feel increasingly pressured to rely exclusively on professional activity in order to imbue their lives with meaning. The messages about our calling, our passion, have been redirected toward the world of work, expanding the idea that a profession is the best place in which to find fulfillment. The goal is to transform work from a necessary burden, an activity that must be performed in order to earn a living, into the central axis of our identity where creativity, progress, and professional satisfaction are key.

The consequences of this shifting social mindset—in the very concept of work itself—are, as we're already starting to see, troubling for a large part of the population that's grown up with this notion that total fulfillment only seems achievable through work. The message we're not getting is that people who manage to work in a field they're passionate about constitute a significant minority.

This is symptomatic of our society, which has enshrined a concept of work associated with happiness and that situates it at the center of our lives, thus diminishing the value of other, more personal aspects of our lives. To avoid disappointment or even disillusionment, it would be ideal to get back to an old-fashioned mentality in which work is a tool for earning a living, not a means of personal fulfillment. Only a few—both in classical as well as modern times—were fortunate enough to find a job with which they felt satisfied. In scarcely thirty years, we've turned the exception into the rule, into the precedence to follow, generating discomfort and distress in all those (and there are many) who don't find themselves "loving" their work.

Historically, work has been seen as a necessary evil, or at least as an obligatory occupation. The goal of a good life was free time, not business. In fact, the Spanish word for "business," *negocio*, comes from the Latin word *negotium*, a compound of *nec*, meaning "not," and *otium*, meaning "leisure." According to the Genesis myth, Adam and Eve lived peacefully in their earthly paradise, enjoying their time together. They didn't have to work to earn a living or put a roof over their heads because the Garden of Eden provided everything they could possibly need. It was as if they had an entire retinue of butlers so they wouldn't have to worry about life's contingencies. But then, suddenly, the lack of freedom God imposed upon them—prohibiting them from eating the fruit of the forbidden tree—became an irremediable desire that would lead to the greatest act of rebellion humanity has ever committed.

A rebellion against their own God, though more specifically against prohibition, against the deprivation of freedom, of the sacred good that, according to the myth, they were unwilling to sacrifice. What's even more interesting is that Eve rebelled against ignorance, placing curiosity, a philosophical attitude, above all else. She had to know what would happen if she bit into the fruit of the forbidden tree. By breaking the divine command, they received the worst punishment: being obligated to work in order to survive.

Ever since the punishment imposed by God upon Adam and Eve—"In the sweat of thy face shalt thou eat bread"—work has been considered evil, the result of having sinned, condemned to labor away with scarcely any free time until the day we die. Looking back on Aristotle's words, we must bear in mind that anyone whose mission is to earn money cannot engage in quality intellectual pursuits. For many centuries, this idea that work was a heavy burden under which there was no pleasure or personal fulfillment to be found remained entrenched in various civilizations. However, with the arrival of the Renaissance, this idea changed thanks to a series of brilliant artists and geniuses who understood that they could, by doing what they loved, earn a good living, be well paid, and gain social recognition. Michelangelo and Leonardo da Vinci did what they were most passionate about in life (though it's true it wasn't always with complete freedom) and also received generous stipends. Much of the current concept of work that's being promoted in today's society is closely linked to this Renaissance ideal. But of course, just as is the case today, these individuals were the exception to the rule, having dedicated themselves to a profession in which creative freedom was absolute. In other words, these are very specific, singular examples. The norm was and always has been to work out of a sense of obligation and to not take any satisfaction or reward beyond the paycheck.

So, then, how did this idea emerge that work dignifies us as human beings? Where does it come from? If we consider that, during ancient times, work was a form of punishment, an obligation that turned someone into a slave, then when did this concept change so drastically into this affirmation that work elevates the individual?

Alain de Botton explains this quite simply in his book *The School of Life*. While we cannot pinpoint the exact historical moment or any cultural precedents, Martin Luther's approach to work represented a shift in the way work was viewed. He had reformed the interpretation of the holy scriptures, and when it came to work, he went so far as to assert that God had endowed people with different gifts and abilities, such that no occupation was of greater value to God than any other. The life of a housewife, a rancher, or a shoemaker could be, in the eyes of God, just as valuable as that of a banker or a religious person who devoted their life to prayer. For Martin Luther, when someone performed a task, they were revealing one of the many facets of God through their labor. We can say that the qualities and talents we possess are granted to us by God so that we can care for one another, and that the way to do this is through our works.

Developing sets of skills dignified people's lives in the eyes of God, who—we must remember—had established laziness as one of the seven deadly sins. The Protestantism spearheaded by Martin Luther was responsible for revitalizing the concept of work, infusing it with dignity, regardless of the type of work a person performed.

At this evolutionary stage of the perception of work, we cannot ignore the philosopher most historically associated with the word: Karl Marx. Marx's concept of "work" wasn't very different from the one Martin Luther proposed. The problem wasn't with the fact that people had to work—this was a given requirement during the Industrial Revolution, which was taking place at the time—and it wasn't primarily about wages either, though fair pay was one of his demands. Rather, it was what Marx called "estranged labor." Work was alienating because it was mechanized, leaving no room for the worker's creativity or personal development. There was no freedom in their work. Instead, they were essentially parts of a larger mechanical automaton not unlike the famous scene in the film *Modern Times* where Charlie Chaplin is tightening bolts on an assembly line.

Under capitalism, work had managed to strip any and all pleasure from the workers, if there was any pleasure to begin with. And, as if that weren't enough, the workers had no right to negotiate their conditions, much less the wage they received. Furthermore, the workers, through their activity—which was all they had of any value, since they owned little if anything else—sold themselves for a wage set by the employer and owner of the means of production. By owning those means, employers didn't have to work themselves, and the product manufactured by the workers was taken by the owners, paid for in the form of a wage or salary, and later sold for much more than what the boss had paid, thus earning him extra profits: surplus value that remained in the hands of the employers.

But with capitalism's advancement in the early twentieth century, and especially with the United States at the forefront, hard work became a social fetish. A coalition of ideas began to spread in which values like honesty and personal worth became linked to one's approach to work. To be a good worker was to be well regarded. Idleness was frowned upon, and indolent people or those who only wanted to do the bare minimum of work needed to get by were labeled as lazy, rejected socially, and were later branded as "losers." The American Dream—this notion that, though hard work, one could achieve one's goals—began to permeate popular ideology everywhere.

Alain de Botton illustrates this evolution quite well when he discusses Katharine Cook Briggs and her daughter Isabel Briggs Myers, who, during World War II, were pioneers in developing the first career-oriented personality assessment: the Myers–Briggs Type Indicator. This ninety-one-question evaluation sought to determine one's personality type and, based on that, recommend a work model in which each individual's potential, talents, and temperament could be useful in identifying and selecting a job suited to the individual's personality. It was a test aimed at finding happiness, personal development, and self-fulfillment through work. In other words, it identified the type of job best suited to each individual and, consequently, guided each individual toward a better lifestyle.

It is interesting that, in this test, money was neither a source of inspiration nor motivation. What was being measured was personal and intrinsic to each person as well as to work. There were no financial associations, which, in part, reflects this notion of working hard day after day, year after year, and achieving the American Dream. Behind this framework lies the idea that, to become rich, you need simply to combine two elements: find the ideal job and work hard at it. Only then can you feel fulfilled.

You're led to believe that money isn't the goal but rather the result of two factors: a job that suits your personality and continuous, dedicated effort. The idea is to convince you that your happiness inevitably depends on this. And to lure you in, you're constantly bombarded with grand, inspiring stories of exceptional individuals who embody this philosophy of life. We're expected to believe that, with these two key elements, we too can achieve the American Dream, and we're presented with examples of some of the great business empires that took these factors into account in order to achieve success. Stories like those of Steve Jobs, Bill Gates, and Amancio Ortega all serve as bait to better digest this philosophy of life in which success is confined and defined by favorable job performance.

The problem is that, today, in the twenty-first century, we're still swallowing it hook, line, and sinker, and the two components that seem obligatory for anyone who wants to be happy have coalesced. The first is to turn your calling into a job and therefore achieve the most coveted motto in the working world: Find a job you love, and you'll never work a day in your life. The second has to do with remuneration: Doing what you're passionate about with perseverance and determination will bring you that much-desired money. These two elements—passion for work and passion for money—seem to be the new cure-all for happiness, which is precisely why we must be extremely careful when embracing those dreams.

TWENTY-TWO

Hephaestus and Aphrodite: Thinking about Merit, or the Merits of Thinking

It would be normal to say that, in a society where capital is the axis around which the world pivots, the way we access that capital would be our central concern. It would be logical to think that job status should be associated with a corresponding salary. But we know this isn't always the case. There are jobs that entail a significant amount of emotional weight and social implications and are also well regarded in terms of social status, and yet they don't necessarily pay well. But the fact that job snobbery exists is associated with an element that has managed to embed itself, unconsciously and unnoticed, into our mindset: the false concept of meritocracy.

If we consider a particular position to be important, it's because we believe there's a real possibility that anyone could potentially attain it. In other words, there's a kind of meritocratic idea in the career hierarchy that makes us think individual merit plays a central role in climbing up that corporate ladder and achieving that next level position. Over the last two decades, we've seen a unique phenomenon taking place in the professional world that's very interesting to analyze: coaching.

Coaching operates in two different spheres. The primary and original one is focused on groups within the business sector. This is where companies hire a coach (or a coaching team) to motivate employees and form a "human team" in which everyone feels like part of a family, gets to know one another, and builds trust with the sole objective of having a direct impact on the company's productivity.

But the other sphere involves the evolution of individualistic motivational coaching. This coaching can be done with personal advisors or—what's more fashionable and widely utilized—through messages about the importance of motivation and effort. In some cases, it can be tremendously harmful to the development of a healthy, balanced personality. We're constantly inundated with countless messages through all possible channels, telling us we have to stay motivated, that our dreams are achievable through dedicated effort, that we have to get out of our comfort zone (rather than expanding and enjoying it), that we focus our efforts on being happy in our professional lives. Because, after all, as the great motivational speakers and gurus say, "We have to find what we're passionate about and dedicate ourselves to it body and soul" if we're going to achieve it.

This implies that people who are motivated and work hard will achieve their goals, but that isn't necessarily the case. I would actually venture to say that, in most cases, this statement doesn't hold true, and that this failure stems from a false notion of meritocracy coupled with a harmful concept of equality. It's akin to saying that everyone has what they have and has achieved what they've achieved because they deserved it. That the primary factor to consider with regard to a person's progression in life is effort, tenacity, perseverance, enthusiasm, and above all, motivation, with a dash of personal qualities thrown in. So, if you haven't achieved a high-end social status or an upper-class lifestyle, then much of the blame for this outcome falls on your own shoulders, because—according to this ideal—we all have the same opportunities.

There's a recurring message that speaks to equal opportunities for all. If that were actually true, then the difference must lie in each individual's merits, in whether or not the individual deserves those opportunities. If you don't develop independent critical thinking skills, these types of messages will get you down on yourself. They can leave a mark, and they can leave you feeling disappointed. These are the kinds of slogans that present people as the sole masters of their destiny, especially when it comes to work and social status.

If we were to simply stop and think for a second, we'd realize that the idea of equal opportunity isn't so straightforward. Being born in a poor environment with a limited set of social and cultural stimuli, being educated in a school in a marginalized district, and living and experiencing that philosophy of life aren't the same as being born and raised in a wealthy, upper-class environment. People in the poor environment don't have the same opportunities as those who grow up in expensive neighborhoods, surrounded by multiple role models, attending private schools with wide-ranging curricula, and belonging to families with generational wealth. Having a strong network of contacts and personal connections is a tremendous help when facing the future.

To this message we can add another that has been circulating throughout human history for more than two thousand years: the idea that work dignifies humankind. Thus, in Hesiod's *Works and Days*, we find phrases as interesting as this one:

> "For the gods keep hidden from men the means of life. Else you would easily do work enough in a day to supply you for

> a full year even without working; soon would you put away your rudder over the smoke, and the fields worked by ox and sturdy mule would run to waste."

This marks the beginning of the Pandora myth, as told by Hesiod, in which the need to work is already acknowledged. A little later on, though, Hesiod himself muses on worker bees in a section called "Virtue and Work":

> "Hunger is altogether a meet comrade for the sluggard. Both gods and men are angry with a man who lives idle, for in nature he is like the stingless drones who waste the labour of the bees, eating without working; but let it be your care to order your work properly, that in the right season your barns may be full of victual. Through work men grow rich in flocks and substance, and working they are much better loved by the immortals. Work is no disgrace: it is idleness which is a disgrace. But if you work, the idle will soon envy you as you grow rich, for fame and renown attend on wealth. And whatever be your lot, work is best for you, if you turn your misguided mind away from other men's property to your work and attend to your livelihood as I bid you. An evil shame is the needy man's companion, shame which both greatly harms and prospers men: shame is with poverty, but confidence with wealth."

Work has always been associated with social status and approval. According to Hesiod's own words, it's through work that one becomes envied. And he also seems to agree with the idea of meritocracy, believing that, through hard work and effort, one could become wealthy and desired.

This isn't the only homage to work we find in Ancient Greece. To give another example, we can turn to one of the most important figures in Greco-Roman culture: Homer. In his *Hymn to Hephaestus* (Vulcan in Roman mythology), he thanks this god for having freed humankind from living in caves and bringing progress through the splendors of labor:

> Sing, clear-voiced Muses, of Hephaestus famed for inventions. With bright-eyed Athene he taught men glorious gifts throughout the world,—men who before used to dwell in caves in the mountains like wild beasts. But now that they have learned crafts through Hephaestus the famed worker, easily they live a peaceful life in their own houses the whole year round. Be gracious, Hephaestus, and grant me success and prosperity!

As if that weren't enough, the very story of Hephaestus seems to support the argument that, by putting in the effort, working hard, and being an expert at what you do, you can achieve anything, even marrying the woman you love. It's been said that Hephaestus, who was born deformed, ugly, lame, and crippled, had a gift for ironworking and was a spectacular blacksmith. It appears that Hephaestus was the son of the goddess Hera (there are three versions of his genealogy; in some, Hera appears as the progenitor who decides to bear Hephaestus as revenge against Zeus, who had fathered Athena alone, while in other versions, Zeus is also considered Hephaestus's father) who, upon seeing such an ugly and deformed baby, hurled him from the heights of Olympus down to Earth. Hephaestus grew up with the Nereids on the island of Lemnos where he learned craftsmanship and how to unlock the secrets of the forge, which ended up earning him his well-deserved fame.

It was he who fashioned all the weapons of the gods. But during his years of learning and training, Hephaestus never forgot the scorn of the gods who had cast him out of Olympus, and he devoted much of his time to plotting revenge. Later, Hera herself, admiring Hephaestus's artisanship and metalworking skills, commissioned a throne of gold and diamonds for her palace. To gain his revenge, he crafted the throne in such a way that, when the goddess sat upon it, she would be trapped there forever. And so it was. The gods pleaded with him to release her, and Hephaestus agreed on the condition that he marry Aphrodite, the goddess of beauty. Zeus granted his wish in order to see Hera freed from her imprisoning throne, and Hephaestus, hideously deformed, married the most beautiful goddess on Olympus, all thanks to his skill and professional ability, along with a bit of intelligent vengeance. Thanks to his merits as a blacksmith and a master of fire, no technical challenge was beyond him. Among the many morals that can be drawn from this mythological history, in our case, we might focus on the idea that social status achieved through hard work can bring you anything you desire, even the woman you love.

Believing that those at the top of the social ladder are there because of their merits isn't exclusive to today's liberal society, and this belief leads to another, much more damaging one. It's the conclusion that, if those at the top are there by merit, then those at the bottom must be there for the lack thereof.

We must switch on our critical thinking skills in order to realize that there are millions of talented people who strive each and every day to move up the social ladder without ever reaching the upper echelon of rungs. This is because the slogan pitched to us from the pulpits of economic liberalism that a successful person is the result of perseverance and talent simply isn't true for most of us. There are many other factors influencing our ability to climb the social ladder over which we have no control: the right network of contacts, the education we received, the endogamy inherent to the human species, a simple stroke of luck. We can't forget the importance of contextualizing each case to situate it in its proper setting and to not let ourselves be fooled by slogans claiming that destiny lies in our hands.

To close out this chapter, please allow me to digress briefly into elitism and snobbery as they relate to the world of philosophy. We often find them when presenting theories. Some philosophers have opted for a sort of professionalization of certain aspects of philosophy. They've decided to study and conduct research solely and exclusively for other philosophers. Their goal isn't to bring philosophical positions closer to society, to help them better understand the world, or to show them what a quality life consists of. These people are the academicist philosophers. They don't try to adjust the intellectual level of their discourses to reach a wider audience; rather, they climb up a mountain from which to expound on their own theories. Anyone wanting to understand them must clamber up to that same professional level. This academicist philosophy has managed to prevail over practical philosophy, generating rejection and animosity among the people, who themselves never found any usefulness in the knowledge these thinkers preach from their tower of wisdom.

Others, though, brought philosophy closer to the people. They came down from the mountaintops, leaving behind the snobbish attitudes they may have once had. Philosophers like Ortega y Gasset, who once said, "I have always thought that clarity is a form of courtesy that the philosopher owes." Or Socrates himself, who only directed his intellectual disdain at those unwilling to reason and who chose not to participate in the sort of intellectual snobbery aimed at those who don't possess the same intellectual abilities as themselves and who wouldn't be able to follow highly conceptualized arguments requiring years of study and a very particular vocabulary, one far removed from common, everyday parlance.

From the moment its practitioners confined themselves to the elitist academic sphere, philosophy detached itself from life, from reality, and started to look down its nose at the rest of us. They ceased to be philosophers and instead became scholars of philosophy, nothing more than mere commentators.

Fortunately, humanity is always in need of guidance and help when it comes to designing models of the good life and how it fits into each historical period. It's precisely for this reason that a part of philosophy—represented by other philosophers—that still exists to this day and that continues to operate at a user-friendly level and strives to be of service to society.

TWENTY-THREE

Amancio Ortega: The Virus of False Hope

The twenty-first century has another problem linked to the false concepts of meritocracy and equality. If the System has managed to convince you that equal opportunity is real and that you're in the same position as anyone else when it comes to achieving professional success and higher social status, then it's entirely likely that you've been infected with the virus of false hope. If you're also convinced that people get what they deserve based on their efforts and qualities, then it's entirely possible that you also believe you can achieve anything you set your mind to in life. Like, for example, being a young, undaunted entrepreneur from a humble family with a standard cultural background adopted by a couple, neither of whom graduated from college, and yet you're still thinking it's possible to become one of those highly successful entrepreneurs, thanks to freedoms, equal opportunities, and your own tenacity, work ethic, and other personal qualities . . . and if you happen to have a spare garage in which to start your business without any additional expenses, well, you're already halfway there. This is the case of Steve Jobs, the famous founder of Apple who is often held up as a paradigm of inspiration.

The distinctive symbols of economic status that once defined social class are disappearing. They've become more relaxed. High-end cars are replaced by mid-range, eco-friendly options. Haute couture clothing is replaced by T-shirts, jeans, and sneakers, and luxury watches have lost their purpose. When the nouveau riche make public appearances, they don't ostentatiously flaunt their economic potential, conveying a false sense of equality. It's somewhat paradoxical that the world's most recognizable cellular device—the iPhone—is used not only by entertainment celebrities, elite athletes with multimillion-dollar contracts, and business moguls, but also by people from lower economic strata who pay monthly installments in order to carry the same object in their own pockets.

This relaxing of the aesthetic symbolism of social classes reinforces the (false) idea of equality that permeates popular belief. It gives rise to the hope that we can be like them, that we can reach the pinnacle of socio-economic success, a hope that's born almost without our realizing it, infecting us through multinational images and messages with which we increasingly identify. In other words, they inject the virus of hope into your very core, and they do it with such masterfully surgical precision that you don't even notice the pinprick.

The System knows full well how much it stands to benefit from the spread of this virus, which has been expanding throughout history, but with the advent of globalization, it has mutated into a more virulent strain. For much of our history, social mobility was extremely limited, and the mechanisms for achieving it were very clearly defined, so the hope of changing one's social status was slim. As such, people placed their hopes in other things such as good health, a happy marriage, or a secure means of livelihood.

The twenty-first century has led us to believe that mobility between social classes is possible, and we even believe this as a fact because we "know" people who have managed to do so. But, of course, when we're talking about "knowing" examples, we're most likely referring to virtual knowledge. If we stop and think—if we flip that critical thinking switch—we'll see how those exceptional individuals who achieved social success aren't so familiar to us after all, even though, at times, it might seem like they are. In fact, if you ask me, we probably know more about them than the people around us.

In this chapter, I'd like to briefly discuss the book *Chavs: The Demonization of the Working Class* by Owen Jones, which presents a complementary theory to our own. According to Jones, the System has made it so that no one wants to consider oneself to be "working class," even if it's true. The stigma of feeling this way is tremendous, which is why we've been led to believe that we are middle class for a very specific reason. First and foremost, perceiving ourselves as middle class adds value because we're not on the bottom rung of the social ladder. And there's an important corollary to this: If we feel middle class, if we believe we're average, the chances of advancement are easier than if we're at the bottom. Upward social mobility feels more within reach. Jones specifically highlights how, in reality, many people who feel and believe themselves to be part of the middle class—measuring this social position by average income levels—are actually lower class. In other words, people who fall below middle-income levels still don't consider themselves low-income. They think, feel, and, perhaps more concerning, they attempt to act as though they're middle class. As such, they live with the hope that one day they'll be able to rise, to improve their situation, because the System has taken it upon itself to present ordinary people who seem to be part of our everyday lives as examples and paradigms of this change.

What happens when you deceive yourself about your social status? Well, by placing your hopes and dreams in a social category that's further away from your reality than you think and feel it is, disappointment, discouragement, stress, anxiety, and perhaps even depression are that much more likely to set in because you're perceiving something as close when it's actually so far away it's all but unattainable. In the meantime, they manage to make you as productive as possible because the virus of hope is driving your belief that you can achieve it.

The System has ensured that we know the stories of successful entrepreneurs like Amancio Ortega who built an empire from scratch. The problem lies in getting young business school graduates to understand that Ortega is the exception, not the new norm, and that their chances of summiting the social ladder through their work is between slim and none. In fact, we're living in such a unique historical moment that it's estimated millennials will be the first generation to have a lower standard of living than their parents. Reality is presenting us with a generation of "mileuristas": workers earning a thousand euros a month, but can barely emancipate themselves.

Since we're not activating our critical thinking skills, universities, business schools, and master's programs keep inviting motivational gurus, speakers, and coaches to reinforce the virtues of hope, encouraging people to continue daydreaming, obsessed with mirages and illusions beyond their capabilities. The virus of false hope has become inextricably tied to the world of work, and this extends to all areas of life: hopes for a happy marriage, delightful children, an incredible job, a spectacular vacation . . .

"Follow your dreams," they say. The American Dream is what they're preaching, and with every passing day it's getting harder to find a vaccine against this particular strain of the virus that's so powerful it can take a debilitating toll once it sets in. And this reality is starting to be sold with heavy-hitting words such as "loser," or, if you prefer something a little more colloquial, "nobody."

Yes, even language itself is mutating in favor of the virus. In other cultures and in other times, it used to be said that life had treated someone badly. In other words, the responsibility didn't fall entirely on yourself, there were uncontrollable external events that forced your life off the path you were expecting to take. In these cultures, the term "unfortunate" is used to indicate someone who hasn't been touched by fortune. But in developed societies like ours, the vocabulary has become aggressive, and the concept of luck is disappearing from our social and professional language. We've ended up replacing the *unfortunate* with the *losers*. But we must not forget that the best tool with which to fight these attacks by a society that manipulates language to the point where its falsifying reality is to use critical thinking.

TWENTY-FOUR

Bertrand Russell: Thinking about Envy and Misfortune

If we feel like failures, we run the risk of developing a series of secondary emotions that won't be of any help when it comes to moving forward with a sensible plan for life. One of the most important emotions that can blow this plan to smithereens is envy. Envy is the manifestation of how harmful and damaging it can be to not activate the critical thinking switch. Envy operates, as we'll see later, in the space between the desire to deny others their goods, pleasures, and happiness, and the desire to possess what others have.

But it leans more toward the former than the latter. If we don't flip that switch, we'll desire what others desire, we'll import the objects of our desires from the outside, and as such, once we've obtained them, our level of satisfaction will be less than optimal. If we wish that the people we know don't have what makes them happy, we'll end up realizing that denying and depriving them of their happiness does not pave the way for our own.

If we add up all the factors we've been analyzing—the idea of a false, doctored sense of egalitarianism, the belief in meritocracy, and the hope that you can reach any rung on the social ladder regardless of your starting point—then it's only natural that one of the most damaging (and dare I say inexorable) emotions in human nature begins to emerge, take root, and flourish: envy.

Thanks to the false notion of egalitarianism, we've managed to increase feelings of envy exponentially. As we've just discussed, great social icons of the business world, like Steve Jobs and Mark Zuckerberg, have fueled this fire—if, perhaps, unwittingly and unintentionally—by appearing in public dressed in the same attire as any of us would wear on an average day.

If we follow Bertrand Russell, we have to acknowledge that "in an age when the social hierarchy is fixed, the lowest classes do not envy the upper classes."

Of course, this doesn't mean we should return to rigid compartments and social immobility. Far from it. But we do need to switch on our critical thinking skills whenever we see billionaires and other highly successful people wearing jeans, T-shirts, hoodies, sneakers, or an ordinary watch in an attempt to present themselves as average people with whom you could identify, thereby falsifying reality.

In the early twentieth century, now more than a hundred years ago, Bertrand Russell wrote the following words on envy:

> "Of all the characteristics of ordinary human nature envy is the most unfortunate; not only does the envious person wish to inflict misfortune and do so whenever he can with impunity, but he is also himself rendered unhappy by envy. Instead of deriving pleasure from what he has, he derives pain from what others have. If he can, he deprives others of their advantages, which to him is as desirable as it would be to secure the same advantages himself."

If we focus on this last point and look at the suicide statistics from developed countries, we are forced to conclude that we aren't approaching the processes of moral, social, and personal education correctly. We must be doing something wrong if people whose basic needs are more than met and have their entire lives ahead of them, yet are so crushed and hopeless that they feel like failures. We're at the point where suicide rates are continuing to rise year after year. Suicide can, at times, be the manifestation of someone blaming themselves for everything that has happened to them, for not having achieved the goals they dreamed about, for feeling professionally, emotionally, or socially defeated. It is the devastating concept of failure as a purely personal responsibility embedded in an unreal void where no external factors, life circumstances, or broader contexts exist.

ENVY 3.0: WHAT FACEBOOK TOOK AWAY

Envy has always been directed at those closest to us—personal acquaintances or others with whom we can compare ourselves or at least somewhat identify with. But with globalization and the use of new forms of social media, it turns out that we've increased the number of relationships—of friends of our friends—so, we've therefore also increased the potential for envy. As if that weren't enough, on these new social media platforms like Facebook, people either distort reality or present it in a very selective way, posting only the most carefully chosen moments showcasing the seemingly wonderful parts of their lives, of their supposedly daily routines. Everyone is laughing, smiling, traveling, having fun, showing off their best looks, best poses, best angles. And, of course, when we open Facebook during the summer months and see all those acquaintances showing off their amazing vacations while you're stuck in Córdoba in 100-degree heat, you're overcome with feelings of failure and discouragement mixed with envy, feelings that crush any attempts to feel good or even content with your own current situation.

Scrolling through Facebook (I use it as a paradigm, an example of this type of social network, but the same applies to all platforms that share this same basic model) requires the critical thinking switch to constantly be in the "on" position. Otherwise, it can be tremendously harmful to our happiness and emotional stability. On May 21, 2017, the newspaper *El País* published an article titled "Instagram: the Worst Social Media Network for Young People's Mental Health," exposing the harm this platform causes when used "mindlessly," generating anxiety and depression.

We all try to present an ideal image of ourselves, our lives, our children, our work. We all try to post insightful reflections, sometimes funny, other times profound. The problem lies in the fact that, when we're using these social networks, we're not analyzing what our friends and acquaintances are posting on their pages. And, of course, with so many people putting their idealized lives on display, we can't help but feel a sense of envy seeping into us.

In the past, you only envied a few people with whom you grew up and were in touch, or maybe some new ones you met along the way and whose realities you'd genuinely come to understand. But things are different now. If we haven't developed the critical capacity to help us analyze and emotionally prepare ourselves to use social media, it becomes a major source of dissatisfaction and envy. That's why it's so important that—if we decide to take the plunge into these platforms or allow our children to do so—we first make sure we're fully aware of what we're going to find there. We have to let reason take the lead over common sense, knowing that what's being put up for consumption is almost always virtual. In doing so, feelings of envy can be at least somewhat stifled.

TOXIC ENVY

If we were to distinguish between different types of envy, we could narrow them down to two categories: healthy and unhealthy. And while these two types are, in fact, nothing more than euphemisms, there are two distinct ways to experience envy. Healthy envy is related to your emotional aspirations: When you feel it, it drives you to achieve the same object or status you're envying.

Healthy envy is simple. You see that someone has achieved something that you'd like to achieve, something you believe and feel is attainable for you, and you set out to do so.

It can occur in two ways. The first is when someone close to you achieves goals you've set for yourself. You witness other people achieving your dreams. In this first sense, if you do ultimately achieve that dream yourself, then your level of satisfaction will be great because you had previously set the goal for yourself. It's a type of envy that doesn't poison you; rather, it can actually bring you immense happiness when you overcome it because you managed not only to equal the people of whom you were envious, but more important, you were able to surpass yourself. It's like when you're training with other teammates to make it to the top division in the league, and one day three of you get called up to the first team. You're ecstatic, and the fact that two of your teammates were also called up doesn't detract from your own success. It's what you've been fighting and training for your entire life. Even when you saw other teammates' numbers being called, you never felt toxic envy. In fact, it was the opposite: admiration.

The second type of healthy envy, which isn't nearly as heartwarming, occurs when you suddenly desire something you've seen in someone else's possession, and until that very moment, you hadn't even considered having your own. In this case, the envy is different, mainly because the object or target of said envy wasn't originally selected by you. It didn't start out as your own long-simmering desire. On the contrary, this object of envy is external. We want to achieve what others have achieved because we believe it will make us happy, that it will make us feel better about ourselves, or maybe we simply want to have or experience for ourselves what other people have, despite never having previously felt a need to have it. Then we set out to reach this brand-new goal, but what we don't know is that, in the vast majority of cases, once you get your hands on it, the level of happiness or sense of satisfaction isn't nearly as high as you expected. On the positive side, this second type of healthy envy serves to boost our self-esteem if we can in fact achieve our goal, though it's not as useful when it comes to gauging the intensity of our happiness and satisfaction because it's a kind of envy that originates from the outside in, not a need that's generated from the inside. In most of these cases, the object of envy isn't what the other person actually possesses; it's the feeling of happiness they're projecting.

The real problem arises when we're suffering from what, in Spain, we call "*envidia malsana*" or "*envidia cochina,*" which is akin to unhealthy or toxic envy. In these cases, the feelings of envy are poisoning you from the inside because you don't think other people deserve their achievements, possessions, the life they lead, the partner they've chosen, the children they have, or the job they do. You think they've simply been lucky because, through the lens you're using to peer into their life, you don't see anything they've done to deserve their current situation, that it was all a simple matter of chance. In other words, you've internalized this toxic envy as the manifestation of an unfair process in which some people have benefited through completely illegitimate means. You feel the balance of effort, merit, and reward have been irrationally and unjustly tipped in favor of people you find undeserving of anything they have. So, in effect, you're envying two things: what they've achieved, and the luck you believe they've had and which was yours. Since, deep down, your belief in the ideas of meritocracy and (false) equality has been shattered, what you begin to want is that those people have their achievements and possessions taken away. You're no longer experiencing envy with the goal of gaining, owning, or achieving what they have.

Now, your petty, toxic envy is centered on seeing those who, according to your standards, don't deserve what they have and should be stripped of it so that you can once again believe in the balance of equality, justice, and meritocracy. So that we can all have the same starting point. This kind of unhealthy envy is focused on the taking rather than the obtaining, on others rather than the self. It's the worst of all envies because it drives dissatisfaction to its highest possible levels.

VISUAL THINKING: THE CASE OF BHUTAN

Envy often uses images as its primary instrument. Social media platforms like Facebook and Instagram use images indiscriminately. With globalization, the power of images has multiplied exponentially, especially when it comes to the pervasiveness of screens. Gilles Lipovetsky dedicates a chapter in his book *Global Screen: From Cinema to Smartphone* to what he calls the "omniscreen." We're surrounded by screens from the moment we wake up until the moment we go to bed. Our daily lives have been overrun by an endless number of screens to which we devote too much attention. The screen around which our lives revolved before globalization—the television—has conceded its throne to the cell phones in our pockets, to tablets, to computer monitors, to the information and advertising on electronic billboards in big cities, to the screens that switch on and off day in and day out in classrooms at our elementary schools, high schools, and universities.

What hasn't come with the proliferation of these screens is the mental preparation necessary for using them correctly. Our way of looking at them has barely changed in terms of visual education, and yet the language has evolved. Depending on the type of display, the format is completely different. This language derives from the intentionality of each screen and the modeling of message transmission. However, this invasion hasn't been accompanied by any educational model with a focus on how to look at screens, on learning how to distinguish the different types of language they utilize. It's not surprising, then, that if we apply the same attitude, attention, and credibility to our mobile screens as we do our computer or television screens, we will be falling into a state of visual incivility, which is becoming increasingly common these days.

We aren't educating screen consumers critically; we aren't training people to approach them with their critical faculties engaged. And the consequences are becoming increasingly evident: Illnesses including anorexia and bulimia are on the rise because, among other factors, we lack the ability to properly analyze images. Depression and dissatisfaction increase when we consume virtual images retouched by artificial intelligence and other computer programs in which everyone seems to be leading idyllic lives.

Images penetrate our cerebral cortex with little if any resistance; they have the advantage of emotionally impacting our innermost selves without passing through any filter that might help us better analyze them. Getting back to the topic of social media, if we don't pay critical attention to what we see on their platforms, we risk suffering the consequences of envy (among many other things), which as we've seen can take quite an emotional toll from us. The board members of social media companies are well aware of the power of images, limiting the available text so that the eye sends the information directly to the emotional center of the brain.

To illustrate the sheer power of the image, we'll look at the nation of Bhutan, which for many years occupied the top positions in global rankings of countries with the happiest citizens. In fact, since 1971, it has been the policy of its leaders to focus on growing Gross National Happiness, rather than Gross Domestic Product. They wanted their citizens to be as happy as possible by strengthening social relationships through national and local holidays, maintaining good public health care, public education, and preserving traditions. On top of all that, the television didn't appear in this small Himalayan country until 1999.

But with the arrival of the virtual image—television—all that was turned upside down. It's symptomatic that even aesthetic and especially cultural tastes changed radically in the blink of an eye, and the citizens of Bhutan began to feel more and more unhappy. Bhutanese women were traditionally strong participants in society, capable of working in agriculture and livestock sectors, working outside of the home while simultaneously managing to support their families. Bhutanese men fell in love with this profile of a woman. But, all of a sudden, they began consuming television. A peaceful society, Buddhist in religion and tradition in its customs, was hit with a tsunami of screens and images for which it was wholly unprepared. The social, cultural, psychological shock was much greater than expected, and within just two years, the country's levels of happiness plummeted as a direct consequence of consuming televised images. Bhutanese men stopped liking their partners, and the aesthetic and social model of a woman became outdated virtually overnight. Men stopped seeing their wives as attractive, and women stopped feeling beautiful when comparing themselves to the models and actresses appearing on their screens.

The power of the virtual image completely disrupted the psychological stability, culture, and model of happiness of a society that had clearly established criteria and values. In analyses of the Bhutan phenomenon, one element often mentioned is related to Buddhist education and the way Bhutanese citizens understood the world. In Buddhism, an image directly generates a desire, and desire creates dissatisfaction until it is fulfilled. Thus, the daily arrival of millions of images broadcast on TV caused among this population a malaise of unfulfilled desires, a wave of unhappiness propelled by the fact they weren't prepared to assimilate the effects of images on screens.

ADMIRATION AS AN ANTIDOTE

Russell offers another solution to avoid getting swept away by feelings of envy: Give up the model of thinking by means of comparison. Instead, we ought to focus on ourselves and the good things that happen to us.

Let's imagine we're on vacation. It might not be on the Caribbean island where our neighbor just went, the cruise our coworker is always talking about, or the beach bar on your friend's Facebook page, but if you're habitually thinking through a comparative lens, then you're not focusing on your own vacation but on someone else's. Maybe you're stuck in Córdoba because financial or other circumstances didn't allow you to go on vacation this summer, so tonight you go out for a few beers at a rooftop bar on the Paseo de la Ribera in Córdoba, enjoying some tapas and the view of the river, having a good time and enjoying some good conversation with friends, your partner, or with your family. The key at that moment is to focus on what you're doing, to enhance the pleasantness of the moment before you, to simply feel good. Ultimately it's about avoiding any comparisons between your situation and those of others doing the same exact thing as you, but on Bolonia Beach or Isla Canela. The habit of thinking in terms of comparisons is a problematic one. As Russell puts it:

> "With the wise man, what he has does not cease to be enjoyable because someone else has something else. Envy, in fact, is one form of a vice, partly moral, partly intellectual, which consists in seeing things never in themselves, but only in their relations."

Russell himself offers the solution to this feeling, so destructive to both ourselves and others. That solution is admiration:

> "Whoever wishes to increase human happiness must wish to increase admiration and to diminish envy. . . . The only cure for envy in the case of ordinary men and women is happiness, and the difficulty is that envy is itself a terrible obstacle to happiness."

It's so simple and obvious: If you want to be happier, all you have to do is flip the critical thinking switch and you'll see things more clearly. Just remember that the habit of comparing yourself with others can be harmful and rarely if ever brings joy into your life. To avoid the tendency to make such comparisons, the best possible exercise is to focus on yourself, seeking out and savoring the good in each and every situation. If you're also able to admire more and envy less, then the path to happiness becomes much easier.

SOCIAL SADISM: GUILT

We must establish a set of priorities, and it's advisable to have as few as possible. To put it another way, it's important to have clear priorities in life, but also to keep them to a minimum and replace futile aspirations with tangible realities. We are people who are constantly making demands—even of ourselves—and we do so all the time. We judge others, sometimes harshly.

The number of demands placed upon us is, in nearly every aspect of life, so high that we're simply unable to reduce this pressure, making us into the executioners of our own identity. The sense of happiness we tend to seek in everyday life becomes superficial because, when we analyze our lives, we focus on the flaws and needs we feel we must fill rather than on our virtues or the satisfaction of what we've already gained or achieved.

Without even realizing it, we've internalized a perfect model of happiness meant for display, and we've set for ourselves an extremely high bar for our goals without considering the harm we're imposing on ourselves. The consequences are widespread; Depression is the most palpable manifestation of this pervading sense of unhappiness. And yet this depression, which stems from a distorted version of self-demand, has a solution, as long as we know how to turn on our critical thinking skills.

Feeling comfortable and at ease with oneself is the foundation of happiness. But what we have to do is distinguish between feeling good about ourselves and becoming a conformist for fear of not achieving our goals. Plenty of people beat themselves up morally and intellectually because they've got in their minds an idealized image of the man or woman they'd like to be, and when they look at themselves in the mirror, they realize how short they've fallen from that ideal. Bertrand Russell asserts that this feeling of unhappiness and misfortune comes from being too hard on oneself, with the ideal they're projecting internally. The only solution, then, is to relax this constant attention on the self and instead shift the focus externally. It's a bit paradoxical that, throughout the history of philosophy, there's been a constant emphasis on the importance of "knowing oneself" in order to achieve a full and balanced life, yet now, in the wake of this bombardment, it turns out the solution Russell proposes for "those unfortunates whose self-absorption is too profound to be cured in any other way" is to have a disciplined focus on the external, on what's outside oneself, diverting inward attention.

When it comes to treating anxiety and depression, one of the primary difficulties patients experience is identifying the root of the problem. In some cases, it's simply the fact that they've been overly demanding of themselves in their efforts to achieve that prefabricated ideal self. These are people who constantly disapprove of themselves because they believe they should be someone different, and they beat themselves up over it day and night. It's not easy to treat this type of person who feels miserable even though, from an external standpoint, that's not how they seem. It's challenging because the battle they must wage is within themselves: the hardest and most formidable of all battles because the goal is to defeat an imbedded ideal born of countless external issues that have managed to gain a foothold deep inside of us.

How can such a harmful image of oneself manage to develop in these people? Most of the time, it's able to sneak in because it hasn't encountered any obstacles in the form of critical thinking. If the switch is activated, it establishes one of the best defenses against the encroachment of harmful ideas that began to percolate within us at a young age, and as we move through adulthood, they become harder to eradicate. The media, the news, and social media are constantly reinforcing the notion of an ideal life, and if they don't pass through the critical thinking filter, they become our constant, toxic companions.

If we find ourselves among those who are constantly feeling miserable, unhappy, or anxious, Bertrand Russell offers us a patently unorthodox philosophical solution: Shift our attention away from ourselves. When the feelings of disapproval and misfortune are directed inward, we must stop navel-gazing and prioritize the external world. In speaking about his own case, he goes so far as to say:

> "Gradually I learned to be indifferent to myself and my deficiencies; I came to centre my attention increasingly upon external objects: the state of the world, various branches of knowledge, individuals for whom I felt affection. External interests, it is true, bring each its own possibility of pain: the world may be plunged in war, knowledge in some direction may be hard to achieve, friends may die. But pains of these kinds do not destroy the essential quality of life, as do those that spring from disgust with self. And every external interest inspires some activity which, so long as the interest remains alive, is a complete preventive of ennui."

That is, in order to avoid the punishing kind of self-obsession that results from never feeling satisfied with our reality, personality, or achievements, Russell recommends taking an interest in what's around us as a kind of therapy.

The problem worsens when we add another factor to the equation. As we start demanding more of ourselves, we will inevitably try to project this demand onto others only to end up judging them by the same standards with which we judge ourselves. It should come as no surprise, then, that they inevitably end up disappointing or irritating us, especially because, in being so harsh with everything regarding our own lives, we end up branding anyone who doesn't share our perspective as useless, lazy, a failure. We often have a hard time understanding that other people can have a completely different philosophy of life, people whose priorities are lightyears away from our own demands, and we make the mistake of evaluating them through the lens of our own work-related or moral expectations.

There's nothing more damaging to a work relationship than sitting next to someone for whom work is the central axis of their life and happiness. Someone who only understands progress and development through professional recognition and success. And if these types of people haven't sufficiently developed their critical thinking skills, they can't help but judge others by their own yardstick. As such, they end up imposing that same, exacting standard of work on everyone around them, falling into a dynamic of rejection and negativity toward those who don't share their work-centered view of life.

But while this can happen to those who pour their effort and personal development into the workplace, it also happens to those who have an equal yet opposite focus. We all know someone who's brilliant when it comes to shirking their duties, someone who has no interest in working but has no choice but to work. This person is convinced their job has nothing positive to contribute to their personal development other than the salary, and not only that, they also try to do the bare minimum required of their duties, dodge responsibilities, and pass the blame onto their coworkers. These individuals, who don't push themselves at work and don't hold themselves accountable, often can't help but judge others by their same low standards. Thus, those who are dedicated body and soul to their job are judged harshly and cruelly. And those who don't share in their concept of work are, in their eyes, either brainwashed, idiots, ass-kissers, or live a pathetic life. Some think everyone is either lazy or useless because they don't measure up to their own standards or aren't as committed as they are, and others believe anyone who's that devoted to their job is nothing but an obsessive pencil pusher. These are two distinct models of people who are equally convinced that everyone else would be much happier or much better off if they would just imitate or internalize their chosen lifestyle.

The best way to avoid falling into either one of these two extremes is to know how to find the middle ground, avoid comparisons, and keep the critical thinking switch turned on. Otherwise, there's an opening through which suffering can take root. We have to understand that our lifestyle doesn't have to be exported to everyone else. In fact, if we're able to grasp the fact that each individual person will have a distinct philosophy of life with a different set of priorities, then we won't be as inclined to get upset when others aren't seeing life the same way we do. The idea isn't to think that our philosophy is best for everyone—that we should impose our worldview on others—but to understand that there are other perceptions and, while we might not share them, we can at least respect them as long as they aren't harmful to anyone.

TWENTY-FIVE

Against Emotional Fragility

We've all heard the phrase "to suffer stoically," but perhaps we don't all know quite what it means. Suffering that isn't voluntarily self-inflicted is painful. Life brings us moments of bitterness and heartbreak, and we have to be prepared for this. To that end, we need to equip our loved ones as best we can. Educating others in happiness and joy seems a simple task (although if we want to take on the project of living a good life seriously, it becomes quite complex indeed), and getting some good news or enjoying pleasant experiences apparently doesn't require much in the way of preparation. However, preparing ourselves for the possible setbacks that life throws our way does require a bit more substance and work, because we can't develop a balanced and, therefore, fulfilling life if we don't know how to confront the issue of pain.

Fortunately, with advances in medicine, physical pain seems to be at least partially overcome or controlled. People like me who have a low tolerance for physical pain have access to a whole host of chemistry that helps us cope with most ailments.

We also know that physical pain is most often temporary, so the anxiety surrounding it is much more relaxed.

What worries us is emotional pain and mental anguish, which can occasionally become something of an irrational fear or an obstacle that seems insurmountable because we don't know how to confront it or how long it will last. We're increasingly less prepared to deal with this type of suffering—just look at the massive amount of research, books, articles, television programs, and educational innovations that are currently focused on emotional education.

Never before have emotions been discussed so much. Never before have we endeavored to understand their inner workings so deeply, and yet we're still incapable of understanding them in ourselves. We're paying so much attention to emotions, and yet instead of mastering them ourselves, we're allowing ourselves to be carried away, manipulated, and controlled by them. Emotions are beginning to dominate human beings, not the other way around. We find ourselves in a state of emotional fragility that keeps us bound to the sentimental plane.

But why so much insistence on educating ourselves emotionally? I feel there's a certain neophilia, or love of newness, regarding this assumption; that is, a tendency to be caught up in what's new. Emotions have become fashionable, and emotional therapies are popping up left and right as the panacea for all problems. An education centered around emotional therapies is becoming more prevalent because rationality requires effort while emotionality feels less demanding.

In our hypermodern society, people demand fast and simple solutions that require little effort, so concepts like critical thinking, the ability to analyze, or the need "to stop and think" aren't easily sold. We insist on emotional education, but always from an agreeable place of comfort. The immediate consequence is a lack of understanding when it comes to negative emotions such as frustration, anger, helplessness, tedium. We're always wanting to experience positive emotions and censor all others, rejecting and avoiding them. The error of these educational models becomes apparent when hard times abound, when sadness and dismay make their appearance.

Other times, though, we suffer more than necessary. I'd venture to say that this is the case more often than not. We can easily be the ones responsible for our suffering, and this happens because we were never taught how and when to "suffer well." As we grow, life unleashes its arsenal of difficult, challenging times, and we're not prepared to fend them off. We suffer because we don't know how to face life with the proper balance when it comes to assessing the intensity of the problems we "think" we have. We suffer from what we might call "potentiatitis": we tend to potentiate, magnify, and exaggerate our problems, categorize them, blow them out of proportion, and end up overwhelmed by the magnitude of it all.

But why this surge in all things emotional? Our grandparents—even our parents—didn't worry this much about emotions. Their world was harsher in terms of comfort, their options were far more limited, and their contact with the outside world was limited to what was close at hand, to what was proximate—in short, to what was real. They tended to accept, as much as possible, the society in which they lived, and they sought out happiness within the limits of their abilities and the reality of their social status. Work was a means of earning a living, and happiness was often amassed unrelated to the economy, in life's personal sphere, completely separate from all things material. On the one hand, accepting this reality came with an air of sadness because it curtailed people's ability to dream about radically changing their situation. On the other hand, they had a fixed starting point and the reality of their life was lived in accordance with it. They sought simple pleasures and enjoyed a more transparent emotional existence than what we're experiencing today.

This growing emotional care empire places special emphasis on education. Current pedagogy emphasizes "educating emotions," as if this had never been done before. In the past, emotions were just one component, something that accompanied homework, content, discipline, and certain expectations. Now, emotions—but only the positive, pleasant ones—are the central axis around which all other factors pivot.

We're witnessing an explosion of new pedagogical methodologies, such as progress-based learning, in which children begin to work on topics with which they feel comfortable and identify. From these new educational pulpits, it is proclaimed that education without positive emotions is simply no good, and teaching strategies are constantly being invented to ensure that children always feel comfortable regardless of their situation at any given moment.

We're falling into what's known as "paedocentrism," meaning that the child is the center of everything. Everything revolves around the child, and—even worse—around their happiness and sense of satisfaction. From their earliest stages, we teach them to foster and nurture positive emotions twenty-four hours a day.

We have to be happy while we're studying, while we're learning, while we're working. We have to feel passionate about what we do at any given moment and in every given moment. But if we can or should learn or teach under the reinforcement and protection of positive emotions, we're manipulating the very idea of real life in which, as we've already seen, there are countless uncontrollable factors capable of filling us with distress, discouragement, disappointment, pain, anxiety, and even depression. In other words, we're forgetting to educate ourselves about suffering.

TWENTY-SIX

Hobbes: Critical Thinking against Fear

Among the many sufferings and concerns we'll encounter in this life, fear will be one of them. Thinking about fear isn't always an easy task, especially since there are as many types of fear as there are people in the world. Each person develops a distinct, personalized, and unique sense of fear, hence the difficulty we occasionally have with understanding the fears of others, particularly when they don't correspond with our own. But we rarely reflect on fear, on its causes (which we sometimes know) or on its consequences (which we aren't always able to foresee). There are notable thinkers who have sought to understand the purpose of fear, and among them I'd like to highlight Thomas Hobbes, who wrote that wonderful phrase, "My mother gave birth to twins: myself and fear."

Sometimes fear is caused by the sadism of someone who wants to make us suffer. Other times it's the irrational, emotional response to a traumatic situation. And for some malicious individuals, fear becomes a weapon of control. As José Antonio Marina rightly points out in his book *Anatomy of Fear*, both Hobbes and Machiavelli agreed that fear is the most powerful and necessary political emotion, the great educator of humanity. Spinoza himself warned that "the mob is terrifying, if unafraid." We are afraid, for example, of losing our jobs, which is why we give in to abusive schedules, despotic bosses, unfair working conditions. We're afraid that our children will suffer—or what might be worse, that they won't be happy—and so we sacrifice ourselves for them to the point where they never learn the value of said sacrifice. We're afraid of being unliked, unwanted, not fitting in, and we're constantly dressing up our personality on social media. When it comes to fear, there are all sorts of colors and flavors.

Professor Marina highlights something essential for distinguishing the various types of suffering: knowing how to differentiate individual fears from collective ones. These are propitious times for sowing fear within the community until it reaches the point of panic. One need only look at terrorist fundamentalism to understand how easy it is, in a fully globalized world, to spread a message and convey irrational, unconscious, and unreflective fear throughout the population. In doing so, it achieves one of its primary objectives: to make us feel unsafe.

Hobbes devotes the first part of his book *Leviathan* to the analysis of human passions, among which is fear. For Hobbes, the natural state of man, when he lived in the uncivilized wilderness, was a war of all against all. In other words, before even considering any sort of agreement with another, humanity was forced to consider the threat of violence, of war, and the fears of others considered his enemies. For Hobbes, humankind is by nature vengeful and proud, and his most important inclination is the desire for power, which holds self-preservation as its final aim.

In its natural state, war becomes the primary source of protection and the means of obtaining power. But when it comes to a lifestyle in accordance with nature, the result can only be loneliness and distrust, because each individual person is driven by natural passions, preventing people from (among many things) living a pleasant life. It is precisely because of this fear that humankind will seek to escape this state of nature, where everyone is everyone else's enemy, in order to sign some sort of agreement or accord providing security. He calls this a "social contract," one of the primary objectives of which is to allay fears and create a sense of safety. Humankind opts for security even knowing full well that it must sacrifice certain freedoms (the law of the jungle, among other things) in exchange for peace and security. But within the security provided by the group, new collective fears will arise. Fears that the economy will crash and we'll fall into a global crisis, that technological progress will result in humanoids taking over the world, that terrorism could strike anywhere at any time. Whenever a city suffers a terrorist attack, fear grips the inhabitants, thus fulfilling the terrorist's objective.

Hobbes defines fear as an aversion, as an effort to distance ourselves from something. It's an emotion of withdrawal, of refuge, of retreating. Fear forces you to withdraw into yourself, to barricade yourself, to "encapsulate" yourself. The goal of all fear is, therefore, to isolate and divide. What could be more ideal for a terrorist than for us to stay locked up in our homes, to stop communicating with one another, or to become suspicious of our neighbors, because anyone could be one of them. If we want to combat fear, this English thinker has a very simple solution to offer us: In the face of withdrawal and isolation, we must counter with outreach and openness.

This is why, when an attack does occur, both politicians as well as the general public take to the streets in a sense of social unity, gathering at the very scene of the violence in order to send a message to the killers: "We are not afraid." We aren't afraid because we've opened up to others, we've broken out of our self-absorbed, encapsulated selves.

When facing our fears, whether individual or collective, we must activate our critical thinking switch and open ourselves up to others, like the small child who, when plagued by horrifying nightmares, goes to their parents' bed only to fall peacefully asleep, feeling the protection of others. It's not about the simple rationalization of fear—something we do often and with little effort—it's about taking action, marching forward, and confronting it by opening ourselves up and reaching outward.

TWENTY-SEVEN

Hellenistic Schools: Instructions for Times of Crisis

What do the so-called Hellenistic schools of classical Greece and Rome (Epicureans, Stoics, Skeptics, etc.) have in common with today's world? They all emerged during a similar time and place, and as Professor Rodríguez Donis points out, their common thread is to provide humanity with peace of mind and a sense of serenity that seemed requisite to the historical period in which they lived: a period of great upheaval and complexity that culminated in the conquest of the East by Alexander the Great. It's important to note that some of these schools, which sought ethical virtue as a lifestyle, were founded by people who lived between East and West. The Stoic school, for example, is said to have been founded by Zeno of Citium, a native of Cyprus, who, like many other Greek philosophers—the famous Pythagoreans included—likely bore Eastern influences. One of the primary topics of research in Eastern philosophy is the concept of the spirit or soul, and if we combine this with influences from the Western Greek world, where reason reigned supreme, we arrive at a very comprehensive vision of the human being and how one ought to face life.

We bring up these currents because I believe the period in which we currently find ourselves shares similarities with them, particularly when it comes to the introduction of new developments and uncertainties.

The Hellenistic schools emerged as a response to a turbulent and changing society that had gone rudderless, lacking the stability of its traditional lifestyles. Today, we're facing a problem that runs parallel to that which the Greeks and Romans already suffered. We find ourselves in a new and disorienting period with regard to the future, a period of chaos and hyperstimulation to the point of saturation. There should be no surprise, then, that movements calling for serenity and introspection are emerging. Yoga, mindfulness, meditation, the proliferation of spas, psychological and educational counseling, group therapy, support groups . . . all are now resources to help people find their direction. A widespread search is underway, and nobody seems to know where to look: a search that has turned self-help books into bestsellers.

Hellenistic schools were being created and expanded as a response to a societal need to seek serenity, calmness, and guidance regarding the historical and cultural context in which the people were living. It was a more than rational response to a complicated historical moment in which the most important thing was knowing how to lead a good life. Today's world is, if anything, even more disconcerting than ever, and yet, despite the emergence of countless therapies, medications, and personal growth, none of these seem to have managed to stabilize people. In fact, with every passing moment, we're feeling more disoriented, more dissatisfied, more frustrated. Depression has already become the leading condition that's shortening human life across the globe. In 2020, it was estimated that one in three people will suffer from it during their lifetime.

Along with hyper-consumerism and disorientation comes a pressing need for reflection and distancing. But what's most in demand is a guide to happiness. This is the central problem facing societies experiencing major paradigm shifts. Globalization and, dare I say, the proliferation of screens coupled with the excessive amount of time we spend in front of them, are two paradigms that have been imposed upon us in an almost authoritarian manner.

Three key elements have emerged as major challenges for confronting the present and constructing a solid identity in the face of what we've been calling—to borrow Zygmunt Bauman's term—a "liquid identity." These challenges are: hyper-individualism versus citizenship or the group; neophilia, which has become embedded as a dogma in which any new thing is assumed to be unconditionally good; and turbo-temporality, which has radically changed the perception of time, such that everything accelerates exponentially, leaving no room for either mid- or long-term planning nor careful deliberations. These three new paradigms through which we've come to view the present have made it significantly more difficult for us to find our direction in life.

Until recently, life had a relatively simple, uncomplicated instruction manual. It may not have held many secrets, but one approached it with a certain sense of tranquil resignation, and within it one found a degree of peace, little in the way of doubt, and above all, acceptance. People were happy in a similar if also more limited way. That's how life was: agreeable, organized in a certain way, oriented in a simple manner, and alternatives were few and far between. As we've seen, people didn't seem inclined to complicate things.

Modern times have shattered the possibility of ever having such an instruction manual. Models for a positive lifestyle are multiplying, and the multiplicity of standards for all of them means we can always find good reasons for supporting any of them. While this openness makes it easier for everyone to find a way to fit in or at least feel a bit hopeful about setting their life project in motion. On the contrary, the lack of a critical analysis of these models leads to significant dissatisfaction and disappointment, much of which is a direct consequence of having an adulterated concept of happiness and pleasure.

The Hellenistic schools sought to identify practical, ethical lifestyles that didn't entail any major complications, guiding life's path in a rational manner where individual freedom was seen as the most precious asset of all. Today, we accept many different life patterns, yet we encounter so many arguments and counterarguments in favor and against them all that we feel lost. While we're given the opportunity to choose from among many different models, we're also encouraged to constantly try new ones, to experiment until we find the one that best fits our profile. The consequence is that we become consumed by the new models, by the new styles, in our quest for the ideal one. The lack of critical analysis centered around our own circumstances prevents us as individuals from identifying what our ideal truly is. Our reluctance to reflect on our philosophy of life leads us into a spiral of experimental trial and error where, at the slightest hint of change, we abandon one lifestyle for another.

STOICISM: THE ART OF COPING WITH SUFFERING

We'll introduce the Stoics by recalling the previously discussed baby experiment, which sought to prove that increased happiness, satisfaction, or pleasure (whatever you want to call it when it comes to babies) occurs when you have control over the situation, when you successfully intervene in what happens in their environment. Stoic philosophy proposes something similar: taking control of your life, and above all, your emotions.

The term itself, "stoic," comes from the place where Zeno of Citium began teaching his lessons in Athens, the Stoa Poikile, which was the portico of the Agora of Athens. It's been estimated that the school of Stoicism remained active for nearly six hundred years, and many of its teachings were taken up and assimilated by younger religions such as Christianity, hence the fame it continues to enjoy to this day. Although both the school and its teachings have faded, their models for life and wisdom continue to serve as examples of conduct and wisdom to this day. Thomas Aquinas was a great admirer of the Stoics and accepted the doctrine of virtue into his conduct. The concept of ataraxia (allowing nothing to disturb one's mood), which we will analyze later, is closely related to the Buddhist concept of nirvana, showing how Stoic teachings also influenced other spiritual life models beyond Christianity. Even Montaigne himself was an admirer of the Stoic Seneca, declaring this when he chose Seneca's *Moral Letters to Lucilius* as a model for his essays.

Of the many lifestyles that could be gathered from throughout the history of philosophy, Stoicism has always been one of the most successful. Not only did it become an ideal for thought and a philosophical theory for those seeking wisdom, it also crystallized into a systematic way of life . . . even for philosopher-emperors like Marcus Aurelius himself.

But why is Stoicism so useful? Because it's a school of life directed toward serenity, calmness, and self-control. It serves to help us when we're having moments of panic, of despair, anger, or rage while at the same time teaching us how to remain composed. Stoicism, as we'll try to explain, can be very useful in terms of providing us with a series of tools that can help us better handle these situations by improving and balancing our mood. For example, when we're feeling overwhelmed by sadness, the normal response is to appreciate comforting words from loved ones. But for the Stoics, this type of relief was counterproductive. Encouraging you, telling you that everything is okay, that it's not that bad, that things will get better is, to a Stoic, simply absurd because offering the consolation of hope makes the situation worse. They advise confronting sadness head-on, not avoiding it or hiding it behind the hope that time will make it disappear, but rather taking control of your life and becoming fully cognizant of it.

As Alain de Botton rightly argues, consolation for the Stoics is like an opiate for the emotions: It numbs them, and as such it must be categorically eliminated. If we offer the calming sedative of hope as a treatment for pain, we're making a mistake. Hope will present itself as another state of mind provoking delusions and continuing anxiety while one waits for the pain to end. To reach inner peace, we cannot numb the suffering with another emotion. On the contrary, hope can cause even greater harm if the desired result never materializes, and rock bottom is hit even harder. We must face pain as it comes—no sugarcoating, no chasers—because we know that, as Marcus Aurelius said, we are stronger than we think. The challenge is that, to uncover this inner strength, we must go through these moments of doubt and pain.

At its core, Stoicism warns us to be prepared, to be conscious that this strength we possess will allow us to successfully confront the setbacks of fate. Things are as they are; they happen without us being able to remedy them, and so we must learn not to think beyond what there is, beyond what is happening, beyond what's present when facing a difficult situation. As Stoics, we must try not to mentally distort either the situation at hand or our own emotional state.

But preparing for these kinds of problems, catastrophes, misfortunes, or other negative events is no easy task, which is why the Stoics advised occasional training in order to be ready for whenever the moment was to arise. Some of the advice they gave included, for example, occasionally dressing in rags or low-quality clothing, sleeping on the floor (they suggested it be the kitchen floor in particular), or eating nothing but bread and water for a day. Extrapolated to today, it wouldn't hurt to occasionally spend some time without technology, without a Wi-Fi connection, without a cell phone, to bike to work instead of driving the car, or take the stairs instead of the elevator. In other words, voluntarily abandoning the comforts of our lives in order to prove two things: first, that we can face life without these same comforts, that we're capable of doing without the things with which we surround ourselves and be fine, and second, that we can value what we possess in its proper measure (not overly so), knowing that, if the day comes when they're not available to us, we can live without them. In this regard, we must internalize the words of Emperor Marcus Aurelius in his book *Meditations*, when he states, "Thou seest how few things are needful for man to live a happy and godlike life: for, if he observe these, heaven will demand no more."

It would be a misinterpretation of Stoicism to reduce it to a mere mental attitude toward suffering in the form of resignation. While it is vital for a Stoic to know how to philosophize in times of misfortune (in good times it's easy), this doesn't mean that Stoic philosophy of misfortune is only for the unfortunate. Quite the opposite. It's not a way of learning to complain and resign oneself to passivity; rather, it's an active struggle against the passions, desires, and possessions that enslave us, against the elements that disturb and disrupt human serenity on all fronts, one of which is fear. The Stoics present their response to the hardest of moments by presenting themselves as fighters unwilling to let go of the most precious good of all: freedom. The freedom to choose the lifestyle that frees them from slavery, from everything that binds them and prevents them from achieving inner peace. The Stoics, like the rest of the Hellenistic schools, ultimately sought, in their own way, to answer the most fundamental ethical question: How should one live?

EPICTETUS: THINGS THAT DON'T DEPEND ON ME

One cannot talk about Stoicism without talking about Epictetus. Epictetus was a slave who became a philosopher and a free man. His real name is unknown, and in fact the word *epiktetos* actually means "slave" or "servant." Epictetus was a slave to Epaphroditus, who granted him his freedom. Epaphroditus, who in turn had been a slave to the famously cruel Emperor Nero (who ordered the death of his mentor Seneca, another Stoic), took care of Epictetus's education and gained his trust, so that he was freed and became a tutor to the emperor. Epaphroditus saw great intellectual ability in Epictetus and nurtured it, having the boy study philosophy under one of the most renowned Stoic philosophers in Rome at that time: Musonius Rufus, of whom Epictetus became the most gifted disciple.

Shortly after Nero's death, Domitian took power in Rome and, in AD 94, issued a decree expelling all philosophers from the capital. At that same time, Epaphroditus was assassinated, and Epictetus had to flee the city, eventually settling in Nicopolis, in western Greece, where he set up residence and founded his own school. There, he gained fame as a philosopher and enjoyed the admiration of the greats, most notably the emperor Hadrian. However, despite all this recognition, he lived quite humbly in a shack that is said to have had no door and was furnished with nothing more than a bed, a table, and a lamp.

Recently, the book *The Present Alone Is Our Happiness* by Pierre Hadot was published; it includes some of Epictetus's teachings. The book begins with one of the core principles of Stoic thought: to view life from two perspectives, the things that depend on me and those that don't. This is the starting point of any model of Stoic philosophy. To be a Stoic, we must be clear about this extremely important distinction so as not to engage in futile battles nor be upset by things outside our control. This separation is all.

We should be clear that there are matters with which we must be very careful; for example, opinions, aspirations, acquired knowledge, and affections. What we cannot control must be quickly identified and not allowed to influence or disturb us, things like opinions expressed on social media: We don't own them, and yet we let them affect us. According to Epictetus, we cannot control what other people achieve or accomplish in their lives, so it shouldn't trouble us more than necessary. In other words, envy can be effectively controlled if we pay no heed to what other people acquire or achieve.

Continuing on with the advice from this great Stoic—advice that we're not always able to accept—we must also be quite clear that other people's affections don't depend on us. We struggle to understand and internalize the fact that we cannot manipulate, control, or otherwise direct what other people do with their emotions and attachments, so it is useless to get frustrated or upset about them. Last, in this string of Epictetus's wisdom, there's a special place for our lack of talent: We must accept that we cannot change it, that we have to welcome ourselves as we are, limitations and all.

This analysis is of particular importance today because we live in an age of excessive optimism regarding the evolving concepts of "success" and "effort." We fail to accept our strengths and weaknesses—especially the latter—understanding weakness as an absence, as a deficiency. We're either unaware of or fail to accept our lack of talent for certain things, nor does society present this reality to us as it is. To achieve inner peace, serenity, and a balanced state of mind, it's essential to recognize that our talents are what they are, that we can train and improve certain aspects of our abilities, but that there are others with which we cannot progress or that we simply don't have.

It's worth remembering that we cannot control—and therefore shouldn't let ourselves be overly affected by—the following:

- People's opinions
- What others might achieve or accomplish
- The affections of others (breakups, neophilia, material consumption)
- Talents we lack

THINGS THAT DEPEND ON ME

So, then, what should we do? Be clear about controlling what depends on us and accepting what comes from nature. For Epictetus, fear and aversion are things that depend on you, so we must learn to avoid them rather than fight them:

> "Remember that desire contains in it the profession (hope) of obtaining that which you desire; and the profession (hope) in aversion (turning from a thing) is that you will not fall into that which you attempt to avoid: and he who fails in his desire is unfortunate; and he who falls into that

which he would avoid, is unhappy. If then you attempt to avoid only the things contrary to nature which are within your power, you will not be involved in any of the things which you would avoid. But if you attempt to avoid disease or death or poverty, you will be unhappy. Take away then aversion from all things which are not in our power, and transfer it to the things contrary to nature which are in our power."

Among the things we can control is one that's of vital importance to these times: our opinions. We must own them. We must form our views as completely and thoroughly as we can, especially because we live in an age of information overload, and before appropriating anyone else's beliefs, it's necessary to analyze the information we're receiving, fact-check it, and establish our own set of criteria so we can forge our own opinions instead of blindly accepting someone else's without prior analysis.

Along with this, a second warning is in order regarding the current trend of sharing opinions on social media, where genuine dialogue is neither practical nor realistic. Platforms like X, where 280 characters barely leave any room for explanation, are used for this purpose. While you can summarize an idea in just a single sentence, it's much more difficult to explain its origin and evolution. Other social networks like Facebook, despite allowing for more text, still fail to get users to devote the necessary time to read it in full, because the need and desire to see other posts mean that posts longer than a dozen or so lines are rarely read in full.

Expressing an opinion for the sake of expression—issuing a judgment when no one has asked for it—can be counterproductive to our future. It's not the first time, nor will it be the last, that an old social media post ends up having consequences in the present. Hence the importance of being true owners of our opinions and the need to know in which circles—and to whom—they ought to be expressed.

Epictetus argued that we should be masters of our inclinations, desires, and fears, but at the same time, we must also control our actions. We must take responsibility for what we do and not get carried away by impulsive or merely imitative behavior. In this regard, he offers us a simple yet meaningful example of how to approach action:

> "When you are going about any action, remind yourself what nature the action is. If you are going to bathe, picture to yourself the things which usually happen in the bath: some people splash the water, some push, some use abusive language, and others steal. Thus you will more safely go about this action if you say to yourself, 'I will now go bathe, and keep my own mind in a state conformable to nature.' And in the same manner with regard to every other action. For thus, if any hindrance arises in bathing, you will have it ready to say, 'It was not only to bathe that I desired, but to keep my mind in a state conformable to nature; and I will not keep it if I am bothered at things that happen.'"

THE TRUE AND THE APPARENT

Equally important in his approach to life is the distinction between what he called "true goods" and "apparent goods." True goods are knowledge, education, morals, and ethics, as opposed to apparent goods, which aren't as essential, things like wealth and social status.

Few things have changed in the last two thousand years, and we've learned only a little. A quick glance at social media reveals that we excessively care about public image, placing a great deal of importance on what we see, read, and hear there. Economic wealth is still desired by every person living in a material world, and it often becomes the primary goal in life. If we look at a recent survey published in the Spanish media about the public figures young people want to be like, the responses are quite telling. It was conducted by the company GAD3 for Educa 20.20 and the Axa Foundation, targeting 12,000 boys and girls between the ages of sixteen and nineteen. The boys placed Bill Gates, Steve Jobs, and Amancio Ortega at the top of their lists, while the girls ranked Amancio Ortega, Emma Watson, and their own mothers. The weight of money and fame remains very significant among the idols of today's youth.

Another key point for Stoics is understanding that life is determined by our idea of it. For Epictetus, life was prescribed by *phantasiai*, by representations. Depending on how we view them, we may feel either more or less fortunate. In other words, there are two ways of idealizing life: the model oriented toward desirable things and the one oriented toward fearful ones. For a Stoic, the way life is lived is greatly conditioned by the idea we have of it.

We must be shrewd about reality because the judgment we make of it always ends up shaping our existence and our perception of the world. If we think people are bad, then we will ultimately distrust everyone and isolate ourselves. If we're convinced that people are selfish, we'll barely be able to establish authentic personal relationships. Therefore, if we want to be happy, we must form an idea of a pleasant life as opposed to a catastrophic one that might befall us if we keep the television on too long. When faced with a challenge, we can always choose between two different perspectives. If we're competing for a job opening or taking an exam, we can consider it a nuisance, a hassle, or we can see it—better yet, we can experience it—as an opportunity to improve. In short, much of my life—how I live it and how I experience it—will depend on the judgments I make about the things that happen to me and those that happen independent of me. This will shape what we might commonly call a bitter person or a happy one.

The Stoics believed that everything in nature is ordered, directed, and governed by a kind of universal law, and that human beings, through reason (a legacy of Aristotle), are capable of understanding it. The idea is to live in harmony with this universal law that governs all, to live in accordance with nature.

An intelligent life is one that finds harmony between what we do and the way we approach life, on the one hand, and, on the other, the things that happen around us and are beyond our control. That is, to be wise means having the ability to understand what's happening around us and, based on that information, to develop a personal attitude that's in accordance with those events.

ATARAXIA: THE ART OF REMAINING CALM

The early Stoics were influenced by the school of Cynicism, especially with regard to politics and morality, but the Stoics who have endured for all posterity are the "New Stoics" or "Roman Stoics," including Seneca, Epictetus, and Marcus Aurelius. It was Stoicism with a moral and religious profile. Stoicism reached its peak during this Roman period because it became a model moral doctrine for behavior within institutions. It was a standard for action when facing problems, both personal and political. In fact, we can safely say that Stoic philosophy, adopted as a model of conduct, served and continues to serve to confront the daily difficulties life presents us with, which is why its reputation and good name remain part of our popular culture through expressions such as "to suffer stoically."

If there's any contribution from the Greek and Roman Stoics that could be of value to the modern world, it's the idea of ataraxia, which can be translated as "imperturbability." But imperturbability of what, exactly? The word is often used in reference to the soul, but here we'll attempt to contextualize it in today's world as the imperturbability of one's state of mind.

It might sound radical, and indeed it is, to attempt to not alter one's mood, but for the Stoics, taking control of one's emotions was essential. Ataraxia must be understood as an ultimate goal, as an end in and of itself—a destination to progress toward, an orienting of life that should be taught from a young age. We know it's impossible to not get caught up in the heat of the moment, the intensity of an argument, or the fleeting passion of a summer romance, but that shouldn't hinder our attempt to lead a life as orderly as possible, seeking the serenity of reflection over the impulsiveness of emotion.

What does this peace of mind consist of? Well, that's exactly it: letting as few things as possible—be they events, people, or circumstances—affect our mood, against our will, I might add. In other words, we have to be masters of our moods. And while it can be quite complicated, that doesn't mean we should stop trying.

The emergence of these Hellenistic schools must be placed in its proper context. They arose during a period when Greece had fallen under Macedonian rule, more specifically to Philip and Alexander, who imposed their own sets of criteria and quelled any potential revolts. These were turbulent times for citizens of Greece. In this regard, the suggestion offered by Maria

Daraki and Gilbert Romeyer-Dherbey (two scholars on the subject) in their book *The Hellenistic World* is apt and insightful. They note that, fundamentally, what the Stoics, Cynics, and Skeptics did was suggest a new or rather an alternative concept to the idea of freedom, one that still resonates today:

> "In contrast to collective autonomy and political action as understood by the Greeks—that is, as a matter for active citizens—both Cynics and Stoics proposed individual autonomy and self-agency."

The idea is of freedom as individual control, freedom as the ability to liberate oneself from the slavery of passion and artificial needs imposed upon us either by ourselves or others. It's the same ideas that Nelson Mandela embodied for more than thirty years: Despite lacking civil liberties while imprisoned, he still felt free in the purest, truest Stoic way.

We would do well to learn the value of this alternative to political freedom. An alternative that consists of possessing the greatest possible autonomy and self-control. Paradoxically, in this world of ours, where democracy has become the prevailing way of life and we enjoy certain freedoms, we find ourselves more enslaved than ever to emotional and material dependencies that prevent us from being happy, dependencies that generate need, though, in effect, we're the ones doing the generating.

With Stoicism, it's important to always bear in mind that we are part of nature and that the ideal is to use it as a reference point with which to guide our conduct in life.

The Stoics' primary ethical doctrine is eudaimonia, which consists of achieving what they referred to as "self-sufficiency" by shedding oneself of unnecessary material goods. It wasn't a pursuit of pleasure per se—at least not sensory pleasure—but rather an attempt to not depend on anyone or anything, especially not fleeting emotions or sensations.

For them, the first principle to follow was to live in accordance with nature. What did this mean to a Stoic? Well, it's actually quite simple. In this, they were influenced by the Greek philosopher Aristotle who, as we've already seen, believed that speech distinguished us from other living beings, and that reason was the instrument for using it. That is, for both Aristotle and the Stoics, what was characteristic of human "nature" was the use of reason. Therefore, when they affirmed that one had to live according to their nature, what they essentially meant was that we had to try to live in accordance with reason, with rationality. This makes perfect sense: Living according to your own nature is doing what you're best prepared for, what you as an organism are best equipped to do. It will be far more appropriate, and indeed simpler, to live according to these dictates of one's own nature. The easiest life would be one guided by thought, which is what most defines us as human beings compared to other living things. Living contrary to nature is not just a mistake, it's counterproductive because it puts us at odds with our deepest means of being.

TWENTY-EIGHT

Seneca: How to Think about Anger

A second postulation or principle that the Stoics clearly upheld was the importance of using reason to distance themselves from their passions. Why? Because in most cases passions provoke restlessness and unease, they cause unrest and are the source of uncontrolled anxiety in our attempts to appease them. Think for a moment about how restless we get when we're waiting for a call, a WhatsApp message, or any sign from a loved one who promised last night that they'd call us today. Or those husbands or wives who, after a stage in their relationship where the passion has cooled, feel tempted by a new coworker who's constantly flattering them and put their lives and marriages at risk by giving in to a passion that had already begun to subside. Or the person who, whether through laziness or apathy, neglects responsibilities at work, putting the person's financial livelihood at risk. Or the slacker of a student who, upon suffering the consequences of idleness, regrets it so deeply that he or she swears never to give in to those feelings again. Or the uncontrollable glutton who, after scarfing down an oversized meal, immediately regrets not having controlled oneself for the sake of health. Or those who, driven by a restless mind, start taking sleeping pills, only to later realize they've become so dependent on the drug that they can't sleep without it.

The Stoics recognized a human weakness for emotions and knew that a significant part of the problem lay in controlling them . . . something that of course required developing significant willpower. But, like any self-respecting strength, this cannot be developed without consistent training.

Among the many emotions that always seem to be rising to the surface, the Stoics focused on understanding and controlling anger. This is likely because some of those who were most representative of the movement were surrounded by people who were prone to intense fits of rage. Seneca, for example, served as the tutor to one of the cruelest emperors in recorded Roman history: Nero. Nero tortured people in his own palace, he enjoyed flaying them, he slept with his mother, and he had a well-deserved reputation for cruel and violent outbursts. Not surprisingly, one of the most interesting treatises this philosopher, from what is now Córdoba, Spain, ever wrote was titled *On Anger.* Seneca apparently directed it toward his pupil Nero, but he had to disguise his intent by dedicating it to Nero's older brother Gallio because he feared the uncontrollable rage of the emperor, who ultimately ordered Seneca to take his own life in front of his loved ones.

Seneca was a great Stoic who escaped at least two death sentences. He knew what his fate would entail because he'd experienced it firsthand. The first sentence was handed down by Caesar, but Caligula's wife argued that Seneca suffered from tuberculosis, that he would die sooner rather than later, and it was therefore pointless to sentence him to death. The second time, he was condemned by Caligula, but before he was executed his sentence was changed to exile. But the one he couldn't escape was the death sentence imposed by his own student, Nero, for conspiring against the emperor. Seneca chose to die by exsanguination, cutting his wrists and ankles in a bathtub in front of his entire family. Unfortunately for him, though, he had to resort to hemlock in the end because, apparently, he wasn't bleeding out enough to result in death.

In modern times, Stoicism can be quite useful in dealing with situations where anger occasionally takes over to the point where we end up erupting. The Stoics believed that anger could be controlled through the use of rational thought. One of the reasons anger arises is due to excessive optimism. We can be overly bullish when forming certain ideas about the world and the people around us. We believe they will act and behave the way we think they should because we've convinced ourselves this is the way it should be. But that doesn't always happen, as anger arises as a manifestation of not understanding a situation coupled with a lack of conformity with it. In general, we lash out at others when they don't share our way of understanding life and confront our beliefs in a way we consider foolish, unjustified, stubborn, or malicious.

Anger appears because we gauge situations, opinions, and other people, thinking that our yardstick should be the same for everyone. We tend to believe that what happens to us, coupled with our way of seeing and understanding the world, should be the same for everyone else. So, when someone isn't able to understand things the way we think they should be understood, we end up getting angry with them or even hating them. This is a mistake. We can't expect others to perceive events, facts, and ideas the same way we do; instead, we ought to consider that others might have very different points of view than ours, or perhaps they are, in fact, wrong, yet simply don't realize it. For the Stoics, people who get angry tend to do so because they're foolish, because they can't think past the tip of their own noses. They believe they're right while failing to understand that others may see things differently or simply be incorrect. And on top of this is a layer of excessive optimism resulting from their confidence that others will interpret life the same way they do.

Intelligent beings (I'm not talking about IQ scores or anything remotely like that) generally don't anger too easily. They don't because they don't expect great things from anyone or anything. They accept that people may misunderstand or that they themselves can even be wrong. They're assured that people are imperfect, irascible, and will occasionally mess up, and as such they're incapable of getting angry at anyone by virtue of being mentally prepared for these moments. Their understanding of the world, of circumstances, and of other people lends them a deeper comprehension of life's setbacks that spares them from suffering.

Anger is often the manifestation of having a misconception about what life is or, rather, how it should be. It arises when something happens unexpectedly, like the driver in front of you making a turn without signaling. This happens when we take for granted that everyone will use their blinkers because we assume everyone knows how to drive—especially because we do ourselves—and we extrapolate this attitude onto what we expect all drivers to do every time they get behind the wheel. But if we've mentally prepared ourselves for the unexpected to happen (someone runs a red light, parks in a no-parking zone, drives the wrong way down a one-way street, or gets stuck in a traffic jam because we're going out for the weekend and everyone else is doing the same), then we won't explode with anger at the drop of a hat. Instead, we'd understand that the world isn't the idealized version of our own self-imposed standards, which, without even realizing it, we're often projecting onto others.

The Stoics also added that the path to happiness involved accepting fate. Ultimately it comes as no surprise that the paths forged by their doctrine trend in these directions considering that, in part, its origin and evolution are directly tied to people who were expats, emigrants like Zeno, who came to Athens from the Middle East, or Epictetus, who was the slave of a Roman patrician. Stoicism began as a way for people who were going through hard times to cope with life and suffering before eventually becoming popular among the most noble figures of antiquity. Some scholars refer to it as the Theory of Resignation, but here the concept of resignation is understood in a positive as opposed to a pejorative sense, thus helping to maintain one's steady state of mind. Whatever happened—the good and the bad—was inherent to the rational part of the world, so learning to resign oneself to it was vital to understanding what the world was like for the Stoics.

When it comes to Seneca, he takes a slightly different stance than do others. He conceives of the Stoic not as a person resigned to the desires of nature who thus ignores them, but rather as a fighter, a person who consciously adopts a warrior's attitude against one's own desires, someone who confronts them like a gladiator, knowing that to emerge from this struggle victorious, one will have achieved a morally worthy life.

This theory of resignation and self-control tell us that, ultimately, everything happens necessarily and cannot be avoided. Why torment ourselves with ideas about how we might have prevented something when these ideas won't change the past? If something wasn't avoided before, it was because it shouldn't have been avoided, regardless of the consequences, so we must accept the unfolding of events as they happened.

Like the other Hellenistic schools of thought, Stoicism is at its heart an attempt to answer the fundamental ethical question:

How should we live? Stoic philosophy is often misunderstood when we think we must rid ourselves of the material goods enslaving us. But that's not the case; neither Marcus Aurelius nor Seneca did this, though they were clear that material goods, while accessible and even useful, shouldn't be given such importance that lacking them would cause us anxiety or discouragement.

This is one of the most valuable contributions to bear in mind for our lives today, in this age of unbridled consumerism where owning, buying, and spending have become hallmarks of our identity. In this twenty-first century, we must learn to keep material things in their proper place, whether it's the cell phone, the computer, the car, or the house. We must develop a doctrine of material detachment that will sink in and take root over time. This is a learning process that can begin during childhood and continue on throughout the course of life. Toys, clothes, brands . . . all these things are trying to convince us they're symbols that define us, and in doing so, they manage to carve out a space in our lives, presenting themselves as actual extensions of us, which is precisely why we need to keep them in their proper place, assigning them no more value than they truly merit.

Stoicism has had great influence as a doctrine of life throughout history, but one of the most powerful examples of its usefulness can be seen in Nelson Mandela, whom we've mentioned before. During his imprisonment, Mandela read and absorbed the Stoic doctrine of Marcus Aurelius, yielded to the course of events, and practiced resignation. When he was released from prison, he decided that what had happened was simply what had to be, and thus he accepted both the fate of his past as well as his destiny. The injustices of the past could not be undone, and as such, they were not worth suffering anymore. During his twenty-seven year sentence, Stoicism gave him the serenity to move forward. After he was released, and after he won the office of South African president, he spoke of peace and reconciliation instead of giving into the anger provoked by the injustices he'd endured.

Some demanded justice for those who had imprisoned Mandela: justice tinged with the subtle thread of revenge. But Mandela accepted the context and circumstances of his imprisonment and chose to embrace it as an element of fate instead of burdening himself with the Sisyphean task of harboring resentment for the rest of his life. Anger is a momentary balm that can, in some cases, leave the bitter aftertaste of rancor for what happened. It's a feeling that runs contrary to the Stoic lifestyle, one that impedes progress down the path toward a balanced sense of happiness.

On this topic, Epictetus once said that suffering does not come from the things that happen to us in life, but rather from the ways in which we interpret and judge those events.

Conclusion

The purpose of this book has been nothing more than to highlight the importance of learning to think well in order to lead a balanced and happy life. Critical thinking is the best tool we have at our disposal for constructing our identity. It gives us the ability to analyze the different contexts we'll encounter through life and to do so based on our own circumstances. It's a built-in, even innate tool, yet we must learn to use it effectively through practice. If we don't, someone else will come along and shape our world for us, while using their own tools to do it instead of ours.

There is an urgent need to adopt an attitude of preventive mental hygiene. We must develop a "maintenance habit" and reexamine our lives every so often. It's no different from maintaining your vehicle: To keep it in good operational condition, we need to get it inspected every so often, change the oil, fluids, tires—that's the only way to keep it functioning properly. If we only take care of the car after it breaks down, any repair is likely to be an expensive one. Problems arise when critical thinking makes an appearance and yet we've never taken the time to develop it. Sooner or later, it demands attention, and if we're not prepared, the result is suffering that feels more like an unbearable punishment.

True happiness is something that's learned, and if we learn it well, it will eventually become a way of being. The hidden beauty of happiness is critical thinking. There's an almost magical harmony when we witness a truly lovely thought, an aura that fills us with an elegant sense of grace and awe. I hope this book has been helpful in showing you how the sublime beauty of a happy life can only be achieved through critical thinking.

Bibliography

Aquinas, Thomas. *Summa Theologica*. Translated by the Fathers of the English Dominican Province. London: Burns Oates & Washbourne, 1921.

Aristotle. *Metaphysics*. Translated by Carnes Lord. Chicago: University of Chicago Press, 1984.

———. *Rhetoric*. Translated by Carnes Lord. Chicago: University of Chicago Press, 1984.

Bauman, Zygmunt. *Liquid Life*. Barcelona: Austral, 2013.

Benedikt, Carl, and Michael A. Osborne. *The Future of Employment*. Oxford: University of Oxford, 2016.

Bermúdez, Manuel. *La culminación del escepticismo en el Renacimiento*. Córdoba: Servicio de Publicaciones de la Universidad de Córdoba, 2007.

Bernstein, Jeremy. *Oppenheimer: Portrait of an Enigma*. London: Duckworth, 2004.

Botton, Alain de. *The Consolations of Philosophy*. London: Penguin, 2014.

———. *How Proust Can Change Your Life*. London: Picador, 1997.

Bouchoux, Jean-Charles. *Les pervers narcissiques*. Barcelona: Arpa, 2016. (Originally published in French; *The Narcissistic Perverts* is an informal translation.)

Byung-Chul Han. *The Burnout Society*. Translated by Erik Butler. Stanford: Stanford University Press, 2015.

———. *The Transparency Society*. Translated by Erik Butler. Stanford: Stanford University Press, 2015.

Campanella, Tommaso. *La città del Sole* (*The City of the Sun*). Madrid: Akal, 2006.

Camps, Victoria. *Elogio de la duda* (*In Praise of Doubt*). Barcelona: Arpa, 2016.

Castilla del Pino, Carlos. *Teoría de los sentimientos* (*Theory of Feelings*). Barcelona: Tusquets, 2000.

Daraki, Maria, and Geneviève Romeyer-Dherbey. *El mundo helenístico* (*The Hellenistic World*). Madrid: Akal, 1996.

Diogenes Laërtius. *The Lives and Opinions of Eminent Philosophers*. Translated by C. D. Yonge. London: G. Bell and Sons, Ltd., [n.d.].

Epictetus. *Enchiridion*. Translated by George Long. Mineola, NY: Dover, 2004.

Gilbert, Daniel. *Stumbling on Happiness*. New York: First Vintage Books, 2007.

Hadot, Pierre, and Epictetus. *The Present Alone Is Our Happiness*. Translated by Marc Djaballah and Michael Chase. Stanford: Stanford University Press, 2011.

Hesiod. *Works and Days*. Translated by H. G. Evelyn-White. London: William Heinemann, 1914.

Hobbes, Thomas. *Leviathan*.

Homer. *Homeric Hymns*. Translated by H. G. Evelyn-White.

Jones, Owen. *Chavs: The Demonization of the Working Class*. Madrid: Capitán Swing, 2012.

Kant, Immanuel. "What Is Enlightenment?" Translated by David Colclasure and Pauline Kleingeld. In *Toward Perpetual Peace and Other Writings on Politics, Peace, and History*. New Haven: Yale University Press, 2006.

Kuehn, Manfred. *Kant: A Biography*. Cambridge: Cambridge University Press, 2001.

Lipovetsky, Gilles. *La felicidad paradójica* (*Paradoxical Happiness*). Barcelona: Anagrama, 2009.

———. *Hypermodern Times*. Translated by Andrew Brown. Cambridge: Polity Press, 2005.

Marina, José Antonio. *Anatomía del miedo* (*Anatomy of Fear*). Barcelona: Anagrama, 2006.

Marinoff, Lou. *Plato, Not Prozac! Applying Eternal Wisdom to Everyday Problems*. New York: Quill, 2000.

Machiavelli, Niccolò. *The Prince*. London: Penguin Classics, 2014.

Marcus Aurelius. *Meditations*. Translated by John Jackson. Oxford: Oxford University Press, 1906.

Marx, Karl, and Friedrich Engels. *The Communist Manifesto*. Translated by Samuel Moore.

Montaigne, Michel de. *Essays*. Vol. 6. Translated by Charles Cotton; revised by William Carew Hazlitt. New York: Edwin C. Hill, 1910.

More, Thomas. *Utopia*. Translated by Paul Turner. New York: Penguin Classics, 2003.

Nietzsche, Friedrich. *The Birth of Tragedy*. Translated by Shaun Whiteside. New York: Penguin Classics, 1994.

Norton, Michael, and Elizabeth Dunn. *Happy Money: The Science of Happier Spending*. New York: Simon & Schuster, 2014.

Onfray, Michel. *Les sagesses antiques* (*The Wisdom of Antiquity*). Paris: Grasset, 2006.

Ortega y Gasset, José. *Meditations on Quixote.* Translated by Evelyn Rugg and Diego Marín. New York: W. W. Norton, 1963.

———. *Meditations on Quixote.* Translated by James Cleugh. New York: Harper & Row, 1961.

Pascal, Blaise. *Pensées.* Translated by A. J. Krailsheimer. New York: Penguin Classics, 1995.

Pinker, Steven. *The Better Angels of Our Nature: Why Violence Has Declined.* London: Penguin Books, 2012.

———. *Enlightenment Now: The Case for Reason, Science, Humanism, and Progress.* New York: Viking / Allen Lane, 2018.

Plato. *The Republic.* Translated by Desmond Lee. London: Penguin Classics, 2007.

———. *The Dialogues of Plato.* Translated by B. Jowett. 5 vols. 3rd ed., revised and corrected. Oxford: Oxford University Press, 1892.

Robinson, Ken. *Finding Your Element: How to Discover Your Talents and Passions and Transform Your Life.* London: Penguin, 2014.

Rodríguez Donis, Luis. *El materialismo de Epicuro y Lucrecio* (*The Materialism of Epicurus and Lucretius*). Seville: Universidad de Sevilla, 1998.

Román, Ramón. *El enigma de la academia de Platón* (*The Enigma of Plato's Academy*). Córdoba: Berenice, 2007.

———. *Pirrón de Elis: Un pingüino y un rinoceronte en el reino de las maravillas* (*Pyrrho of Elis: A Penguin and a Rhinoceros in Wonderland*). Córdoba: Servicio de Publicaciones UCO, 2011.

Russell, Bertrand. *The Conquest of Happiness.* New York: Liveright, 2013.

Schwartz, Barry. *The Paradox of Choice: Why More Is Less.* New York: Ecco, 2004.

Seneca. *On Anger.* Translated by John W. Basore. London: William Heinemann, 1928.

———. *Ad Lucilium.* Translated by Richard M. Gummere. New York: G. P. Putnam's Sons, 1917.

Shelley, Mary. *Frankenstein.* London: Penguin, 2005.

Spinoza, Benedict. *Ethics.* Translated by Edwin Curley. New York: Penguin Classics, 2005.

Zimmer, Robert. *Basis-Bibliothek Philosophie: 100 Werke aus zwei Jahrtausenden* (*Basic Library of Philosophy: 100 Works from Two Millennia*). Stuttgart: Reclam Verlag, 2001.

DOCUMENTARY

Bollaín, Icíar. *In a Foreign Land*, 2014.

FILMS

Allen, Woody. *Deconstructing Harry*, 1997.

Chaplin, Charles. *Modern Times*, 1936.